Edited by Philip Long and Jane Thomas

BASIL SPENCE
ARCHITECT

National Galleries of Scotland in association
with the Royal Commission on the Ancient and Historical
Monuments of Scotland

Royal
Commission on the
Ancient and
Historical
Monuments of
Scotland

Heritage
LOTTERY FUNDED

Arts & Humanities
Research Council

The Scottish
Government

Published by the Trustees of the National Galleries of Scotland to
accompany the exhibition, *Back to the Future*: *Sir Basil Spence 1907–1976*,
held at the Dean Gallery, Edinburgh from 19 October 2007 to 10 February
2008 and at The Herbert, Coventry from 20 June to 31 August 2008.

ISBN 978 1 906270 00 1

Designed and typeset in Univers and Futura by Dalrymple
Printed on Furioso 150gsm by Die Keure, Belgium

Front cover: Coventry Cathedral, detail from the south east of the
baptistery and nave windows, 1961
SC1029530 RCAHMS

Back cover: Basil Spence's house at Beaulieu, Hampshire
SC1076430 RCAHMS

Frontispiece: detail from London Midland Railway poster showing a
drawing by Spence of the new Coventry Cathedral, 1957 [see **26**]
DP021470 RCAHMS

The proceeds from the sale of this book go towards supporting the
National Galleries of Scotland.

www.nationalgalleries.org

FOREWORD

This book and the major exhibition that it accompanies are the result of the gift of Sir Basil Spence's archive to RCAHMS – one of Scotland's national collections. The archive was donated by the architect's family and we are extremely grateful to them for their generosity. From the outset it was clear that the archive had considerable potential to contribute to a greater understanding of our architectural, sociological and artistic heritage. Not only did the range of the material suggest new ways in which the collections of RCAHMS could be made more accessible, but also by working with another of Scotland's national collections – the National Galleries of Scotland – a major project could be undertaken that would result in an exhibition of the work of one of Scotland's most creative talents. Basil Spence, more than any other architect of his generation, combined excellent and forward-looking design with a love of the visual arts, and, where possible, integrated murals, sculpture, tapestry, textiles and other applied arts into his projects. This characteristic alone suggested that a partnership between our two organisations would be highly productive and so it has proved.

Under the banner of the Sir Basil Spence Archive Project, work has been undertaken to conserve, catalogue and make the archive collection available both by direct consultation and through digital access. A further partnership with The Lighthouse, Scotland's centre for architecture, design

and the city, has resulted in an innovative nationwide educational programme, which is being presented through a touring exhibition in 2007–8. With the assistance of the Arts and Humanities Research Council another publication is underway, which will take the form of a comprehensive source book recording and describing the architect's projects.

This book provides new insight into Spence's life, career and projects, and has been written and prepared by several of the experts who have been closely involved with the research for the archive project and the exhibition. We would like to express our gratitude to them and to our numerous colleagues for advising, cataloguing, conserving, researching and undertaking educational and promotional work on the project's behalf. Finally, we would like to thank most warmly the Heritage Lottery Fund and the Scottish Government, whose generous funding, support and advice have made all the contributing elements to this ambitious project possible.

John Leighton
Director-General, National Galleries of Scotland

Diana Murray
Secretary, Royal Commission on the Ancient and Historical Monuments of Scotland

Portrait of Basil Spence, c.1950
SC1027537 RCAHMS

INTRODUCTION

Sir Basil Spence was for many years the most prolific and celebrated architect of his day, yet in recent times his place in the story of twentieth-century British architecture has been largely overlooked. The year 2007 marks the centenary of his birth and this gives us the opportunity to assess his legacy through the buildings themselves, a great many of which have survived, and through the design material from his office archive that has entered the public domain.

No other British architect contributed such a range of work to the public building stock and it is a tribute to Spence's ability to engage with a brief that so many of these structures are still in use for the purpose for which they were designed. In the post-war period alone, he designed a nuclear power station, an airport, a crematorium, the first of many of the country's new university complexes, a cathedral, an embassy, an army barracks, exhibition pavilions, schools, churches and a range of municipal housing schemes. As well as this extraordinary range of public work he also carried out many commercial and private domestic commissions at home and abroad.

It is not only the volume and scope of Spence's work that makes him worthy of reassessment, but also the considered way in which he introduced modern ideas into his schemes. In 1961, the *Daily Telegraph* recognised that: 'by his Coventry Cathedral design and his work for the Britain Can Make It exhibition and the Festival of Britain, Sir Basil Spence has probably done more than any other architect to make the contemporary idiom acceptable to conservative public opinion'. Clearly this was not an approach that found favour with radical architects of the time, or indeed more recently to architectural historians in thrall to Le Corbusier and the international modernists. Spence was certainly interested in the work of the Bauhaus and experimental designers working in Britain and overseas, to the extent that he incorporated a visit to the exhibition of contemporary houses at Weissenhof Siedlung into his honeymoon. He also made sure to visit Le Corbusier's chapel at Ronchamp soon after its completion, lecturing to the Royal Institute of British Architects about it on his return. Although Spence was particularly enthusiastic about the work of Mies van der Rohe and Frank Lloyd Wright, he also championed two architects who were deeply out of fashion in the 1950s but who are now considered to be highly significant, namely Edwin Lutyens and Charles Rennie Mackintosh. Whilst he was inspired by such figures, Spence was pragmatic in the use of radical ideas in his own work. His architectural training at Edinburgh College of Art was a traditional one and gave Spence the ability to mediate between progressive and mainstream approaches with great success.

Had Spence carried out no other work than Coventry Cathedral, this building alone would justify a prominent place for him in Britain's post-war design story: he masterminded and oversaw the creation of one of the key symbols of post-war regeneration. This complicated project continues to resonate today, having been voted Britain's most popular twentieth-century building in the 'Buildings of the Century' national millennial poll. From the moment he won the competition, ahead of 218 applications, to design the cathedral in 1951, to its consecration eleven years later, the building was to dominate Spence's life, occupying half of his career spent working in England, and providing a unique training ground for many distinguished architects of the future.

Spence was a household name, a gifted communicator who popularised the subject of architecture to the post-war 'brave new world' generation through interviews on the radio and television, lectures and articles in the press. He took on this role willingly partly because of the need to keep the public informed about progress at Coventry but also to help raise extra funds for its completion. His book about the genesis of Coventry Cathedral was a best seller. Spence was also a passionate advocate of his profession who, as President of the Royal Institute of British Architects, not only helped to modernise the organisation itself, but went to great lengths to promote architects and their work to the general public. He was knighted, awarded the Order of Merit by the Queen, the Médaille d'Or by the French Government and myriad honorary degrees and awards by organisations throughout the world. The most visible architect in the

Hutchesontown 'C',
Gorbals, Glasgow, 1965
SC1052317 RCAHMS

country, it was inevitable that he should attract criticism. With the benefit of hindsight we are able to revisit his work and judge for ourselves.

A vital part of reassessing Spence is the availability of his office design archive, which has recently become publicly available thanks to the generous donation of his family. We are very grateful indeed to Gillian and Anthony Blee, Sir Basil Spence's daughter and son-in-law for their help, support and advice and for their very personal contributions to this book. We would also like to thank Spence's former colleagues, who have been unfailingly generous with their knowledge. The Arts and Humanities Research Council has provided a grant supporting academic research on Spence, and we would like to acknowledge the essential contribution this has made. We also wish to acknowledge the considerable support given by the Sir Basil Spence Archive Project Steering Group, chaired by Professor John Hume. This book and the exhibition which it accompanies are inextricably linked and we would like to thank the following for their important contributions to both, and in particular those who have lent to the exhibition: Professor Louise Campbell (University of Warwick); Geoffrey Clarke; Elizabeth Cumming; Robert Drummond; Professor Brian Edwards (Edinburgh College of Art); Miles Glendinning (Edinburgh College of Art); Jo Hibbard (Coventry Cathedral); Judith Legrove; Tim Pethick and colleagues (Studio SP); Joseph Robson; Charles Hind and Lucy Rowe (RIBA British Architectural Library Drawings and Archives Collection); Roger Vaughan and Ron Clarke (The Herbert, Coventry). Finally, we would like to thank our numerous colleagues at the National Galleries of Scotland, the Royal Commission on the Ancient and Historical Monuments of Scotland and The Lighthouse, who through working together have made the Sir Basil Spence project possible.

Jane Thomas
Curator, Royal Commission on the Ancient and Historical Monuments of Scotland

Philip Long
Senior Curator, Scottish National Gallery of Modern Art

Basil Spence posing for a press photographer at the drawing board in his Edinburgh office, *c.*1950
SC1048956 RCAHMS

BASIL SPENCE ARCHITECT

LIVING WITH SPENCE

GILLIAN BLEE

My father died over thirty years ago, and it is difficult to retrieve chronological events from the scrambled-egg of memory. As I write this, I can hardly believe that more than a quarter of a century has gone by without his vibrant presence. He was passionate, energetic, wonderfully funny – and at times, especially when my brother and I were young, quite frightening. He would look at you with those grey-blue piercing eyes of his, and you knew that he was not pleased with a particular action or word. But those times were few and far between and my overwhelming memory of him was his unbounded enthusiasm.

He was an architect first and foremost. He had a deep love for his profession. Perhaps this was, in part, because it was difficult for him to train at Edinburgh College of Art because of lack of money. It was imperative for him to win the year prize in order to continue his studies. One way of supplementing his income was to draw architectural perspectives for others. I believe the fee for these works was calculated by the square inch. He always maintained that was why his enormous skies were so proficiently painted – less building, more sky – a better return for effort! He was a brilliant draughtsman. I remember him, tongue tucked into the side of his mouth in concentration, sketching with pencil or unsuitable pen (many of his sketches have faded) or tackling a vast architectural drawing at enormous speed. Being an entirely practical man this would be on a board propped up with whatever was to hand – often a brick or two. It was only latterly that he graduated to an all-singing, all-dancing parallel-motion drawing board.

My father was also a painter and sculptor of talent [1]. His vibrant use of colour was, I believe, a recognition of the sights of his childhood. He was born in India and lived there until he was twelve. One can only imagine how difficult the change must have been for him, leaving his mother and father and travelling with his younger brother to a country completely different from all that he had known, exchanging the incandescent Indian light and colour for the grey stone and silver light of the Scottish capital.

My early memories of him are very dim. He enlisted in the Army in 1939 before war was declared, as he had spent his honeymoon in Germany in 1934 and was very concerned by what he experienced there at that time. I do remember the first bomb in Scotland landing in our garden, and the huge crater it made – what excitement! We, the family, travelled around with him until he left with his Camouflage Unit in June 1944 for France and the Normandy beaches.

He returned in December 1945 laden with presents. In fact, when he arrived home with other demobbed soldiers the cry went up 'Here come our boys!', then, spotting my father with his flowing moustache, 'and here comes Father Christmas!'

It was wonderful to have him home, and my mother, brother Milt and myself, having recently returned to Scotland from Devon, settled into our new life. This was the time of the exhibitions – Enterprise Scotland, Britain Can Make It, British Industries Fairs, and others – culminating in the Festival of Britain. He was busy, but there was always time for his models. I remember many a cold morning at some reservoir or other testing the latest model boat that he had designed: the excitement as the boat cruised across the water, the drama as it hit an object or did not perform as anticipated. It was boats then; later he started building aeroplanes. To us children it was all enormous fun. Before the war he had built a huge model railway with shunting yards, signal boxes, stations, all surrounded by a backcloth of the most romantic Scottish scenery. This was a passion that never left him. Much later he used to throw pebbles up to his six-year-old granddaughter's window at some unearthly hour in the morning, in order to wake her up to accompany him on yet another test flight.

From the age of thirteen to eighteen I was at boarding school just outside Edinburgh, so I only saw my father during the school holidays – but what holidays they were! Every summer we went abroad in whatever car we had at the time. It is difficult to describe in this era of mass-travel how exciting even the word 'abroad' felt. Equal weight was given to the roadside picnics and the architecture [4]. I'm not sure which are clearer in my memory, Corbusier's Ronchamp or

1 Basil Spence at Dar Tal Ghar, Malta, 1972
Private collection

those wonderful caves at Lascaux, or the cold watermelon, delicious cheeses and raffia-encased red wine. Our 1951 summer holiday was very special. My father had won the competition for the new Coventry Cathedral in August, and our family holiday had been arranged for later that month. We were to drive to Spain where we were to spend time on the virtually empty Costa Brava. We visited great cathedrals on our way south with Dad sketching at every stop. He was tired and emotionally drained, and the holiday could not have come at a more important time. While we were at our hotel he painted four interiors and one exterior of the new cathedral, all critical steps to the final built design. Not being one to sit around on beaches – or in fact, to sit around anywhere – he was always doing something, usually painting. On our holiday in Portugal in1959, he left us gazing at the great rollers of the Atlantic, while he wrote the first draft of his bestseller *Phoenix at Coventry* – and we were only there for a fortnight!

After a period at Drama College, I decided that the stage was not for me, and enrolled at Secretarial College. I think that my father saw my potential and offered me a job as his secretary. I jumped at the chance of working closely with him. This was in I955 when the Cathedral project was in full flow as well as various other projects such as three small churches near Coventry, a school at Sydenham, Thorn House and the University of Durham Physics building. At this time my father was heavily involved with the Royal Institute of British Architects (RIBA); he became President in 1958. It was exciting to work for him; he was an enthusiastic, energetic and demanding employer. His involvement with artists on nearly every project was particularly interesting: Geoffrey Clarke, Keith New, Lawrence Lee and Alan Davie made visits to the office, and there were meetings with Graham Sutherland and Elisabeth Frink, and visits to Jacob Epstein's studio. It was a cosy situation, as I was living at home, and the office was downstairs, but this was also very efficient, as I could be called on day and night.

My father's term of office as President of the Institute

was very successful. The *Guardian* architectural correspondent wrote in 1962: 'Sir Basil's genial personality enabled him to raise his voice demandingly, persuasively, aggressively in the cause of a better environment nearly every day of his two years in office.'

In 1956 the office was overflowing in our small Georgian house in Queen Anne Street and we moved to the lush greenness of Canonbury, Islington. As usual we lived above 'the shop'. The office was a small design team of young enthusiastic architects, many of whom went on to make their mark on the profession. Amongst these was the young Anthony Blee, whom I married in Coventry Cathedral in February 1959 [3]. After my father died one of the architects who worked in that office wrote to my mother: 'My time in his office was, by a long way, the happiest of my life. Not just a kind man, but an inspiration – and you, who gave us your house to work in and your garden to play in, we all love because you were his wife, and half of him.'

My father and mother met in London when my father was working in Sir Edwin Lutyens's office. They were a formidable badminton couple; in fact they were a formidable couple. My mother was fiercely loyal and supported him in every way. My father described her as 'the reinforcement in the concrete'. What is certain is that he would not have achieved all he did achieve without her amazing common sense, wit and intelligence [5].

Theirs was a long and happy marriage, the last years being spent at their beautiful house under the Dingli Cliffs in Malta and then in Suffolk, a county they always loved. With typical energy, although he was already ill, my father tackled the conversion of Yaxley Hall with gusto. It all seemed to be finished in a trice – house, garden and a new summerhouse [12]. This was his last building, and I can see him now watching the structure being winched into place and turning to me and saying, 'that looks about right'. Three days later he died.

When we came to decide what John Skelton should carve on his gravestone there was no discussion. Basil Spence Architect – that said it all.

2 Basil, Gillian and Milt Spence, at 14 Jordan Lane, Edinburgh, 1947
Private collection

3 Basil and Gillian Spence on her wedding to Anthony Blee, 1959
Private collection

4 Basil, Joan and Milt Spence on holiday in Italy, 1948
Private collection

5 Basil and Joan Spence, 40 Moray Place, Edinburgh, c.1948
Private collection

6 Sea and Ships Pavilion, Festival of Britain, London, 1951
Private collection

WORKING WITH SPENCE

ANTHONY BLEE

In May 1973, Mary Banham, the wife of the famous critical writer and architectural commentator Reyner Banham, came to the office at 1 Canonbury Place in the course of her research while writing her book on the Festival of Britain, *A Tonic to the Nation*. She was delighted to be shown the model of the Sea and Ships Pavilion, which we had kept in a garden shed that doubled as our print room.
By that time the model was twenty-three years' old and looked it! It transpired that this was the only surviving model of a pavilion for the festival. Mary offered to have it restored, if we would agree to donate it to the Royal Institute of British Architects Archive. Basil readily agreed to that proposal.

This gift represented our first donation to an archive, while our recent gift to RCAHMS of the Sir Basil Spence Archive has fulfilled our wish to secure the proper conservation of, and public access to, much of the important evidence of Basil's life and work. We had been storing it for the twenty-six years since Basil's death at the age of sixty-nine in 1976.

The composition and sequential experiences of the Sea and Ships Pavilion represented a masterpiece of innovative thinking and spatial dexterity that anticipated the work of the design practice Pentagram, but has not been sufficiently recognised as having done so. For me, the Sea and Ships Pavilion was by far and away the most exciting part of the entire exhibition in 1951, and influenced me so profoundly that I resolved to study architecture [6]. The exhibition which accompanies this publication offers an opportunity to re-evaluate that scheme and many other ground-breaking achievements, built and unbuilt and some already demolished.

The year 1951 was a special year for Basil for another reason. That was the year in which he won the competition for the design of Coventry Cathedral, the drawings for which were produced while he was still living and working in Edinburgh.

As a final year architectural student in 1955, I was preparing my dissertation on the subject of 'Religious Expression in Modern Architecture'. That research inevitably prompted me to seek an interview with Basil Spence in order to learn more about his work at Coventry. I met him for the first time in his Queen Anne Street office. As I entered his room on the first floor, I was astonished at the enthusiasm with which he showed me, a complete stranger and mere student, what he had been working on that day. I noticed how the side of his drawing hand, which had been in contact with the paper, was black with carbon pencil, his sleeves were rolled up, there were wet paint brushes in a jam jar on the mantle shelf, and the drawing which he had been working on had just been unpinned so that he could show it to me. It was a study for an amendment to the design of the cathedral porch. He asked me my opinion of the change. Fortunately, I was able to identify what had been changed. Maybe he was testing me. In any case, I felt flattered to have been asked. I immediately felt as if I was involved.

When at last it came to my search for full-time employment for my professional practice, I was fortunate enough to be offered jobs in all the London offices to which I had applied. But it was my recollection of the Sea and Ships Pavilion, together with the prospect of participation in the development of Coventry Cathedral that decided me. I joined the office when it was still relatively small, but shortly afterwards Basil realised that it had become too busy and crowded for him to continue living upstairs. His move to Canonbury in Islington with a small contingent from the Queen Anne Street office enabled the formation of a design studio in rather more peaceful surroundings [7]. Initially, architects from the other London office in Queen Anne Street and the Edinburgh office would come to Canonbury for short periods of time and take scheme designs back with them. But the core team, in which I was fortunate enough to be included, stayed in Canonbury to work on the most prestigious projects.

The office was characterised by its youthful vigour and skills. When Basil visited university schools of architecture, to lecture or to examine, he was able to spot student talent and recruit them. Equally, students at the point of graduation would frequently approach him, seeking work. His growing international reputation meant that there was a steady flow of job applications, many from overseas. As a consequence, the staff in the office at times included architects from the USA, Canada, Brazil, South Africa, Germany, Ireland, Egypt, Greece, Poland and Australia.

The atmosphere in the studios was delightfully informal, not unlike that of university architecture schools at that time. Tea and lunch breaks tended to become protracted with spirited conversation. The camaraderie and enduring friendships, as well as romances, evoke happy recollections. Basil's daughter, Gillian, and I were the first couple to be married in the new cathedral, while it was still under construction.

We applied ourselves not only at our drawing boards and in model making, but also competitively out of the office on the cricket pitch and tennis courts. We played against other architects' office teams as well as against engineers and quantity surveyors.

Basil was undoubtedly the creative inspiration and mastermind of his offices. But the practice of architecture on a large scale requires the input of numerous qualified professionals in several disciplines and is essentially a team effort. For example, Basil's personal friendship with that great engineer Ove Arup meant that Arup's took part in all our projects [8].

Basil's own pattern of work was awesome in its complexity. His demanding public engagements, especially during his term as President of the RIBA, took him out and about so much that he was prone to get back to his drawing board late into the night and at weekends. That is why he always chose to live with his family immediately above or beside the office, so that he could maintain contact with us at short notice and monitor what was being drawn up. He had a habit of prowling around the boards at dead of night, inspecting what we had been doing and even leaving tiny sketches with cryptic notes: 'Not this … but this!' Then he would return to the quiet seclusion of his own studio.

Basil found the quintessence of the atmosphere in which he liked to design at a sequence of retreats outside London. There he could think and work, or relax and pursue his hobbies of sailing and model making. Typically, he would receive a commission, research the programme, visit the site and then escape to 'the cottage' at a weekend, where he would apply himself with absolute concentration, returning with an amazingly finite set of proposals. Before long, he would have worked up and refined the scheme, dealing with such

flaws as he had identified through further consideration and discussion in the office or with the client. I was fortunate enough to witness and even to share in much of that genesis, spending weekends and holidays with him, in the family fold.

Holidays, particularly in the Mediterranean, saw him designing, painting, sketching, model making, cooking and socialising – he was indeed a bon vivant. His travels are well-recorded in his sketches, rapidly executed with the pad on his lap, and often smoking a cheroot to aid concentration. These trips informed his work to a significant degree.

Back in his studio in London, he would seek to show exactly how a new design would appear when built. He had a habit of setting up one or maybe two perspectives to a small scale, but extremely accurately, then, overlaying the set-up with tracing paper, he would take a charcoal pencil and test the viewpoint, bringing the image to life with bold shadows and by hatching in the tonal values of the various materials. Having 'proved' the particular viewpoint and light source in this way, he would set up the final image to a large size on paper using a hard pencil and then fully render it with watercolour washes, pastels, gouache and charcoal. Because of his superb technical and artistic virtuosity, his clients were able to anticipate what their buildings would look like and how they were going to function. And if they wanted to be reminded of what Basil had in mind for them, when travelling with them in a train or plane, he would grab the nearest piece of paper (on several occasions this would be a BOAC airline sick bag) and he would rattle off a quick sketch using a felt pen with astonishing fluency and graphic clarity. He had a disarming habit of giving away such sketches, so those in the exhibition are rare survivors or have been retrieved on loan from the present owners.

Basil's concerns, however, extended far beyond such beguiling images. Every sequence of spaces and every detail had to be considered and designed: he would say that one judges a good building as one judges good tailoring – at the seams. He was as interested in the furniture and fittings as in the overall concept. In certain respects his philosophy can be identified with that of the Arts and Crafts movement. He also believed that there should be a place for art as an integral part of a building, not merely as an afterthought. Hence his close collaboration and friendship with great artists of the time.

While Basil was undoubtedly the creative inspiration and

7 Basil Spence at his drawing board at Canonbury Place, London, with the model of the British Embassy, Rome, 1964
Private collection

8 Basil and Joan Spence with Sir Ove Arup at the official opening of the British Embassy, Rome, 1971
Private collection

9 Basil Spence and Anthony Blee on the terrace at Spence's house, Beaulieu, Hampshire, 1961
Private collection

mastermind of his offices, partners and staff participated fully in the production of the detailed documentation, the negotiations with clients and planning authorities as well as the supervision of construction contracts. Furthermore, there were occasions when architects within our office initiated design solutions.

In later years, the other offices in turn became autonomous. The twenty-year period during which I worked ever more closely with Basil saw the Edinburgh office progressively 'going it alone' while his original (ex-Edinburgh) London partner, Andrew Renton, set up his own practice at the Queen Anne Street office as Renton, Howard, Wood, Levin. Later, there was a similar separation with the departure of John Bonnington, who had been with us in Canonbury, and then had been Basil's partner running the Fitzroy Square office with Gordon Collins. Ultimately, Basil and I were to remain as partners at the Canonbury office, having already seen the consecration of the cathedral and several churches as well as the completion of several university projects.

We managed to stay relatively small in terms of staff numbers in Canonbury, although when Basil and Joan moved to live in number two Canonbury Place the office expanded upstairs to fill number one. The overseas work, in Rome (the British Embassy), Cannes (luxury apartments), Amsterdam (offices), Athens (bank headquarters) and the Middle East (offices, law courts and cultural centre) meant that we posted staff from Canonbury to branch offices in those locations and occasionally engaged local staff. For Basil and me this meant many exciting challenges and an extremely demanding travel schedule, especially between 1968 and 1975. In fact it was on one such trip – to Bahrain in 1975 – that Basil fell ill and I had to get him home urgently. That was his last overseas journey.

It had made sense for Basil and Joan Spence to have a base in the Mediterranean, first in Majorca and then in Malta [10]. That meant that overseas site visits could be linked to sojourns in those retreats. Latterly, Basil was travelling further afield, to Australia, New Zealand, Canada and the USA. I used to chauffeur him to and from Heathrow Airport, which gave us time on those journeys for a briefing. The first thing that he wanted to know was if anything had gone wrong in his absence. It would also give me the opportunity to raise issues on new developments, new projects and to prioritise whatever needed to be studied in greater detail when we got

back together in the office or over the weekend [9].

There were many landmark events which I find noted in my diaries, such as toppings-out [13], consecrations, formal openings (often royal ones), inaugurations, new commissions and honours – all mixed in with family celebrations such as births, birthdays, anniversaries. Basil adored his family and always made time to join in. He even involved his grandchildren in model making, commissioning them to make palm trees at three pence a piece to be used on the Bahrain model, his last project.

The honours of his knighthood, appointment as a Royal Academician and Royal Designer for Industry, the treasured Order of Merit and the French Académie d'Architecture Gold Medal reflect the great esteem in which he was held both at home and abroad.

10 Dar Tal Ghar, Malta, 1971
Private collection

11 Dovecote, Broughton Place, Edinburgh, 1936
Private collection

12 Tea House of the August Moon, Yaxley Hall, 1976
Private collection

13 Basil Spence on the roof of the British Embassy, Rome, during the topping-out ceremony, 30 May 1970
Private collection

EVOLUTION OF A PRACTICE

JANE THOMAS

Sir Basil Spence was the best-known British Architect, almost the only one known to the general public. The centre of many controversies, a passionate defender of his works, he was always news and on his death on 19 November last year (1976) even television reports covered his life and works. There would be no doubt a national figure, a 'Great Architect' has died.
Sir Frederick Gibberd, *Architectural Review*, January 1977

Through public recognition and myriad honours awarded both in Britain and abroad, Spence achieved his ambition to 'get on'[1] in his chosen profession. This desire to succeed carried him further than the dream of his expatriate parents, whose focus was a homeland that neither they nor, indeed, his grandparents had experienced in reality. He was brought up in a community steeped in abstract nostalgia: 'Edinburgh is the most beautiful city in the world. I remember hearing this first at the age of seven when, with my family, I was in India [15] and the legend of Edinburgh was firmly upheld by Scottish families there.'[2]

A feeling for his Scottish roots was fostered at the John Connon School, established by the Bombay Scottish Education Society in 1881, as a precursor to experiencing a genuine Scottish schooling when he was sent to George Watson's College in Edinburgh at the age of twelve [16]. Excelling in art at school led naturally to enrolment at Edinburgh College of Art, where his drive to win as many awards and prizes as possible [20, 21, 22] was influenced by a degree of financial hardship at home. Although the family was never affluent, money became particularly problematic when Spence's father died in 1927[3] to the extent that the College approved a maintenance scholarship of £40 'in recognition of the unusual brilliance of his first year's work' so that he could continue with his studies.[4] Financial pressure also undoubtedly influenced his willingness to sell his artistic skills as a perspectivist to interpret the designs of prominent Scottish architects such as Leslie Grahame-Thomson (1896–1974) and Reginald Fairlie (1883–1952) [19]. His student life was also supported through being appointed as a junior lecturer, despite the fact that he was still a student in his diploma year at Edinburgh College of Art, because the college felt his work was so advanced. He was to continue teaching in various capacities at the college until 1939.

14 Basil Spence with a selection of perspective designs for exhibitions including (centre) the Council for Industrial Design stand at the Scottish Industries Exhibition, *c.*1949
SC1048956 RCAHMS

15 Basil Spence in India, aged four, *c.*1911
Private collection

16 Basil Spence (left) and his brother Gerald wearing George Watson's College uniform, *c.*1919
Private collection

Once established in practice with William Kininmonth (1904–1988), Spence was in a position to propose to Joan Ferris, with whom he had been corresponding for five years, ever since meeting her when he was working in Edwin Lutyens's London office on the Viceroy's House, New Delhi. They married in 1934 and honeymooned in Germany where they visited the Weissenhof Siedlung at Stuttgart [17], an exhibition of houses designed by architects who were to become key figures in the modern movement, such as Le Corbusier (1887–1965) and Walter Gropius (1883–1969). Although the exhibition had been held seven years before the couple visited, it was still intact enough to be an extremely stimulating experience for an architect at the outset of his career.

Spence was in partnership with William Kininmonth for eight years before joining up for active service in World War Two. On his return to Edinburgh he set up his first practice, Basil Spence & Partners in 1946. Reflecting on his career before this point he later said 'I realised that the work I was doing before hadn't the proper base, no direction about it.'[5] His family had occupied various rented houses while Spence worked with Kininmonth in an office in Rutland Square, Edinburgh, but by 1948 home and office were combined at 40 Moray Place, a large townhouse in the heart of the city's New Town [see 5]. Whether or not this was influenced by his time in the Lutyens's office, over which the architect and his family lived, the logistics were similarly organised, with the office and draughtsmen downstairs and family upstairs, and a rigid distinction maintained between the two. Although Spence had a studio in the home part of the building, this was for his personal use, and meetings were always held downstairs in the office. It was an arrangement that suited him because 'As my life is architecture, it is natural that part of my home is given over to studios.'[6] However, in the future, as time inevitably became more constrained, he was never again to have the luxury of a room devoted to his train layout, as he had at Moray Place.

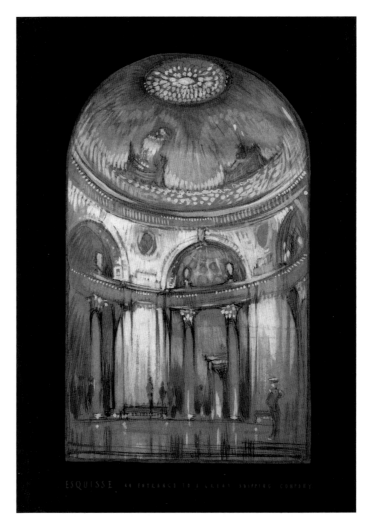

17 A photograph taken at Weissenhof Siedlung, Stuttgart by Spence while on honeymoon, 1934
SC1063403 RCAHMS

18 Student *esquisse*: 'Entrance to a Great Shipping Company'
DP011890 RCAHMS

19 Perspective by Basil Spence for Reginald Fairlie's alterations to St Salvator's Church, St Andrews, 1929
DP5B502 RCAHMS

THE · SOANE · MEDALLION · 1931 · 32 ·

THE · ROWAND · ANDERSON · STUDENTSHIP · 1930 · 1931 ·

NATIONAL · INSTITUTE · OF · ARCHITECTURE

20 Basil Spence's design entry for the Soane Medallion competition, 1931–2
DP021047 RCAHMS

21 Basil Spence's winning entry for the Rowand Anderson Studentship, 1930–1
DP012734 RCAHMS

22 Basil Spence's design entry for the Pugin studentship, 1931
DP016900 RCAHMS

The way in which Spence organised his domestic and office accommodation was to set a pattern for the rest of his career, as was his management of the design process in the office. It was rooted in the training he had received at Edinburgh College of Art, which was in turn based on the way in which the École Nationale Supérieure des Beaux-Arts in Paris taught architecture. Established in 1795, the 'Beaux-Arts' approach placed great importance on the development of drawing skills. A key aspect was the production of an *esquisse*, a pictorial representation of a design solution, as the first stage in responding to a brief [**18**]. Speed was an important part of the process in which an *esquisse* had to be conceived and executed within twenty-four hours. Throughout his life, Spence would consider a design brief over a short period of time, usually during weekends, returning to the office with a design solution, often with a perspective for the client to communicate his response to what was required.[7] This was an important part of his skill at salesmanship, an aspect of the profession which he admitted relishing.[8] The speed and flamboyance needed to work successfully in this way contributed to his success as an exhibition designer to the extent that, prior to his work on Coventry Cathedral, it was for exhibition work that he was primarily known. His talent in this area was recognised both in 1948, when he was awarded an OBE, and in 1960, when he was elected a Royal Designer for Industry (Exhibitions and Interiors) by the Royal Society of Arts.

Commissions were hard to come by in the 1940s and Spence, like many Scottish architects of the time, looked to England for work. His work south of the border began in 1947 with commissions for two local authority housing estates, including Sunbury, for which he was awarded a Festival of Britain housing award in 1951. As his work in England expanded, home and office life were split for a while, leaving the family living above the Edinburgh office during the week while Spence worked at his newly established office at 29 Buckingham Street, London.

Winning the competition to design a new cathedral for Coventry in 1951 [**25**] inevitably had a dramatic impact on home as well as office life, precipitating the family's move to London the following year to live over the office once more, this time at 48 Queen Anne Street. Eleven staff were employed at this point but soon the increasing amount of work relating to Coventry, in addition to a growing volume of university design work, meant that many more staff were needed. In 1956, the year in which the foundation stone for Coventry was laid, Spence's staff more than doubled and so an additional office was opened at number one Canonbury Place, Islington. Spence established his home and head office at the latter, moving to number two as the office grew, but otherwise remaining in the same street for virtually the rest of his life [**27**].

Given the way in which Spence liked to retain creative control of the design work, splitting the offices resulted in a sense of hierarchy in which the Canonbury office, the 'generating house', took precedence.[9] In practice, this worked by Spence producing plans and elevations to a small scale in the Canonbury office and then passing them to the Queen Anne Street office to be worked up in more detail. It was inevitable that staff would sometimes feel excluded from the creative part of the process and a compromise was established for some projects whereby the job architect would work up Spence's design with him at the Canonbury office before returning to Queen Anne Street to work on the final detailing. Partners and staff from the Edinburgh office would come down to consult on key jobs as Spence no longer had time to visit Scotland.

As the number of jobs carried out by the practice increased, so did Spence's role in public life. Coventry Cathedral was a project for which the general public felt a unique sense of ownership, and Spence responded to this by devoting himself to lecturing, appearing on radio and television programmes to discuss the cathedral's progress and travelling to fund-raise for its completion [**24**]. He also invested a great deal of time in the architectural profession during his time in office as President of the Royal Incorporation of British Architects (1958–60), not only by trying to modernise the institution in terms of the service it provided to its members but also in raising its public profile. In both these capacities, he sought to mediate the architectural design process to a wide audience at a time when the British Government was engaged in a range of ambitious building programmes aimed at expanding the country's public housing stock and improving access to educational opportunities, so that 'for a time the country was aware that architecture was important and absorbing'.[10]

The public role that came with designing Coventry Cathedral, a symbol of Britain's regeneration, was one that Spence undertook with a strong sense of responsibility. However, as the staggering volume of press attention

23 Spence's sketch
perspective of Coventry
Cathedral from Priory Street,
*c.*1953
DP020043 RCAHMS

24 Basil Spence
demonstrating a model of
Coventry Cathedral as part
of his lecture on architecture
for young people at the Royal
Institute of British Architects,
3 January 1955
SC865991 RCAHMS

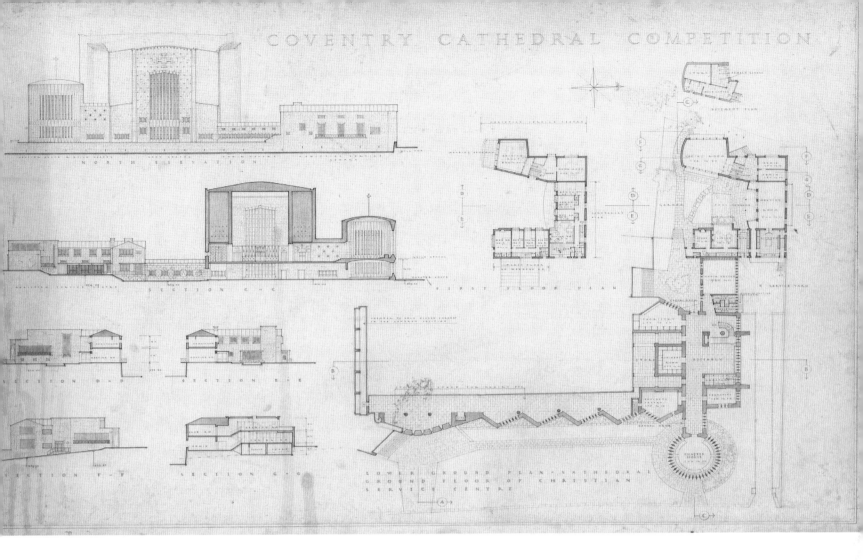

The rebirth of Coventry Cathedral

The Cathedral Church
of St. Michael of
Coventry — The porch

Coventry is served by the London Midland Railway

25 One of Spence's Coventry Cathedral competition entry drawings, 1951
DP012295 RCAHMS

26 London Midland Railway poster with a 1957 drawing by Spence showing the porch of the new Coventry Cathedral and the ruins of the old cathedral
DP021470 RCAHMS

27 The drawing room of Basil Spence's home and office in
Islington, London. On the wall is the full-scale test piece for Graham
Sutherland's Coventry Cathedral tapestry, and in the foreground is a
table designed by Spence, c.1960.
SC1048362 RCAHMS

28 Basil Spence outside his Canonbury office in the 1950s
SC1048958 RCAHMS

29 The weekend home Spence designed for himself at Beaulieu, Hampshire, 1961
SC1024755 RCAHMS

30 The interior of Spence's house at Beaulieu
SC1072917 RCAHMS

illustrates, his role grew from that of a spokesman communicating the progress of the building to the giant collective client that was the nation, to becoming, in effect, the chief promoter of the concept of architecture to the general public. Part of this sense of duty to the public was demonstrated by his willingness to lecture to as many organisations as his punishing schedule would allow. He also devoted a significant amount of time to various committees of the Civic Trust, Royal Fine Art Commission, Royal Institute of British Architects, Royal Academy and the Building Centre Trust.

The late 1950s were particularly pressured, with work on Coventry drawing to a close and a growing need to address the tensions between the London elements of the practice. It was during this time that Spence began work on his second home, having secured a site beside the Beaulieu River in Hampshire [**29, 30**]. Undoubtedly Scandinavian in spirit, it was not dissimilar to the Aalto House, designed by Alvar Aalto in 1936, with its white painted brick base and dark timber upper storey. Open plan, with space for his boat and a workroom below the living area, it provided a refuge for sailing, designing in peace and a great deal of socialising with family and friends.

By 1961, the division of work between the three different offices and the relative autonomy of the partners resulted in a dissolution of Basil Spence & Partners. The consecration of Coventry Cathedral in 1962 proved a watershed for the practice, which was subsequently able to concentrate on other projects rather than the one that had dominated it for a decade. Spence retained the office at Canonbury with Anthony Blee as his partner, renamed as Sir Basil Spence OM RA, to reflect his newly awarded Order of Merit and his status as a Royal Academician. He valued the OM particularly highly since it was the personal gift of the Queen. Former partner Andrew Renton carried on independently at Queen Anne Street as Andrew Renton & Associates while the Edinburgh office of Spence Glover & Ferguson remained within the Spence practice. Many large and complex projects were now in hand, including eight universities, two civic centres in London, Glasgow Airport and the British Embassy in Rome. The need for a second London office was pressing and so 1 Fitzroy Square was opened, soon after which, in 1963, John Bonnington and Gordon Collins from this new office were taken into partnership with the establishment of Sir Basil Spence Bonnington & Collins. Within

two years, this new office had seventy-five staff working primarily on the large university projects while the twenty-four staff based at Canonbury concentrated on prestige projects such as the British Embassy, Rome and Hyde Park Cavalry Barracks in London, both of which had a complex gestation and took virtually the whole decade to complete.

The gloomy financial climate of 1970s Britain proved a testing time for architects, with much less work to compete for than had been the case in the 1960s. Many firms, including Spence's, sought work abroad, particularly taking advantage of the Middle East oil boom. Spence spent increasing periods abroad at his second home but continued to act as a consultant for the three practices. He necessarily diversified away from the type of public projects which had occupied most of his career, so that commercial and consultancy work dominated his last few years of work, largely for the Hammerson Group but most controversially when he acted as consultant for Fitzroy Robinson on the redevelopment of 50 Queen Anne's Gate, London as a large office building later occupied by the Home Office, on a site from which a large block of Victorian flats had to be cleared. His final project, however, illustrated that his creative powers remained

31 Basil Spence during construction of the British Pavilion at Expo '67, Montreal
Private collection

32 The design model for
Spence's last major project,
a Cultural Centre for Bahrain,
1976

undiminished when he produced an accomplished, if unexecuted, design for a Cultural Centre for Bahrain [**32**].

In recognition of a life lived largely in the public domain,
Spence's death was formally marked with the singing of a
Requiem at Coventry Cathedral on 11 December 1976 and
a service of thanksgiving for his life at St James's Church,
Piccadilly, a few days later.

In a career largely spent designing public spaces, Spence
spoke often in the media of the architect as a servant of his

clients[11] but perhaps what typifies his underlying belief
in the purpose of his role is contained in his advice to the
pupils of his former school:

You should demand a beautiful background for your own
lives. Beauty is thought and sensitivity and feeling. It doesn't
cost more. Sometimes it costs less because one of the ingre-
dients of beauty is simplicity. The background that you demand
for yourselves is the fabric of your own lives, the enclosure
for living.[12]

33 Basil Spence's perspective for the Southern Motors Garage,
Causewayside, Edinburgh, 1933–4
DP004289 RCAHMS

FIRST BUILDINGS 1932–9
ARTS AND CRAFTS TO MODERNISM

CLIVE B. FENTON

In his pursuit of success, Basil Spence was always single-minded as if there was much to do and little time to do it. When he was choosing his career, articled apprenticeships for architects still existed but Spence took the quicker route as full-time student at Edinburgh College of Art (ECA), which he entered in 1925. There, he threw himself into his studies, collecting an astonishing number of prizes.

The college, which had been founded on Arts and Crafts ideals, taught a variety of subjects, including architecture and sculpture, but drawing was the core skill of every subject and Spence excelled at this from an early age. His interest in art and handicraft seems to have been inherited from his mother and encouraged at secondary school by his art teacher, Ralph Hay, who was enthusiastic about various media, particularly engraving, and lino and woodblock printing. Spence's own woodcuts owe much in style to Hay's symbolist work, although even then Spence favoured architectural subjects. His first published works were woodcuts in the school magazine then, as a student, his drawings appeared in the journal of the Royal Incorporation of Architects in Scotland (RIAS). Consequently, architects, such as Reginald Fairlie [see **19**] and Frank Mears, commissioned him to prepare perspectives of their designs.

Before discussing a selection of buildings from the first decade of his career, it is necessary to consider both Spence's milieu and his influences. Edinburgh College of Art architectural students studied construction, mechanics and materials at technical college, while at the art college there were courses in sculpture, colour, and the history of architectural development from classical Greece to the Renaissance, including a lecture on Scottish architecture, which examined 'the traditions of modern architecture'. History informed design, and students were asked to produce compositions based on classical and medieval elements before moving on to exercises responding to contemporary needs. They also made detailed sketches and prepared measured drawings of buildings they had visited. Spence received high marks for history, free-hand drawing, and perspectives.

Many of his friends at college had strong architectural connections. His fellow architecture student Kenneth Begg was the son of the Head of Architecture at the college, John Begg, while Hugh Lorimer, who as a student turned from architecture to sculpture, was the son of architect Sir Robert Lorimer (1864–1929).[1] In 1927 Spence sketched medieval and Renaissance buildings in Northamptonshire with Begg and the following year visited Normandy with Hew Lorimer.

William Kininmonth knew Spence slightly from school and college, but they became friends in 1929 when Begg secured places for himself, Spence and Kininmonth, in the prestigious office of Sir Edwin Lutyens (1869–1944). Lutyens had made his name as a designer of country houses and gardens, but his largest and longest running commission was for the imperial capital of New Delhi, for which he embraced the classical style on a monumental scale. The importance of fine materials, workmanship and attention to detail was stressed, and he employed a large number of assistants to help produce detail drawings. Lutyens had a great impact on the three student architects and his practice may have served as a model for Spence's in his later rise through the ranks of the profession. The young Scots were put to work on the Delhi commission, then approaching its conclusion.

The trio also attended Albert Richardson's evening lectures at University College London. Richardson (1880–1964), an enthusiast for Georgian architecture, had been trained in the Beaux-Arts tradition, in which design was led by rigorous planning and ordered by classical language. Richardson was one of the few British architects of his generation to acknowledge the need for a modern contemporary architecture, and favoured a pared-down classical style. Spence came to share Richardson's preoccupation with the reconciliation of modernism and tradition.

Even before he completed his studies, Spence was teaching at Edinburgh College of Art. In 1930, he was appointed junior assistant instructor, helping to fill the void left by the architectural authority John Summerson (1904–1992), and spent the rest of the decade teaching there, while at the same time establishing himself in practice. Summerson had made his presence felt in Edinburgh with his advocacy of the modern movement, which he regarded as a phase in architectural history as important as Gothic or Baroque, and 'a vital thread in the weft of modern civilization'.[2] In addition to his teaching, he edited the quarterly publication of the Royal Incorporation of Architects and made an appeal in *The Scotsman* for British architects and patrons, whom he regarded as twenty years behind the times, to catch up with and embrace the new style and the principles of Le Corbusier. The consequent debate in the letters page demonstrated some hostility to the importation of foreign ideas and disdain for the affectations of mechanical motifs applied to buildings.[3]

Once he had his diploma, Spence's entire architectural career was spent as a partner or principal, never an assisant.

His first partnership came when William Kininmonth invited Spence to join him in practice.[4] The architect A.F. Balfour Paul (1875–1938), by then sole partner in Rowand Anderson & Paul & Partners, let them use a small room at his Edinburgh Rutland Square premises and they started in business in late 1931, sharing a drawing board in a room containing little but a typewriter and telephone.

According to Kininmonth, his practice was founded on the basis of two Edinburgh commissions [**34**, **35**], from Dr G. Grant Allan and Dr John King (both were business partners of Kininmonth's radiologist brother).[5] Suburban houses for the Edinburgh professional classes provided the core of the practice's modest amount of early work. At that time Scotland was struggling to recover from the economic

HOUSE AT CRAIGLOCKHART
FOR DR. AND MRS. ALLAN.

34 Design for a house at Craiglockhart, Edinburgh, for Dr and Mrs Allan, 1931/2
Private collection

35 Lismhor for Dr King as published in *The Architect and Building News*, 23 August 1935
Private collection

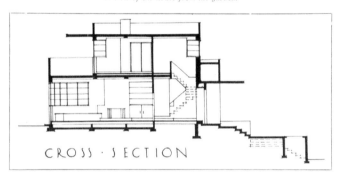

August 23, 1935   THE ARCHITECT & BUILDING NEWS   227

A view of the house from the garden.

CROSS · SECTION

ROOF · PLAN   GROUND · FLOOR · PLAN

House for Dr. King, Murrayfield, Edinburgh.   Architects : Kininmonth & Spence, AA.R.I.B.A.

depression of the late 1920s and early 1930s and money was scarce. Of necessity, private practice took second place to teaching for Spence until at least 1935. He was, however, aware of the value of publicity, promoting the firm to the press and ensuring that their designs appeared in every annual exhibition at the Royal Scottish Academy. Meanwhile, Spence's student sketches of medieval architecture in Northamptonshire and Normandy continued to appear in the *RIAS Journal*.

In the early days, Spence and Kininmonth worked on the same drawings, although Spence generally did the presentation perspectives. Kininmonth seems to have begun designing Dr Allan's house, at Craiglockhart, before Spence joined – his name alone appears on drawings dated May 1931.[6] But Spence produced the perspective of this substantial Lutyensesque house with ogee roofs, monumental chimney stacks and a rather Romanesque entrance. The early Kininmonth & Spence houses are variations on a theme: brick construction, white-painted render, tiled roofs, window shutters, and sometimes bowed windows. Economy was always an issue and the architects attempted to provide architectural detail without additional cost. One method, perhaps learned from Lutyens, was to insert roof tiles between courses of brickwork used to emphasise an archway or a fire-surround.

Dr King received building consent for his house, Lismhor, at Easter Belmont in May 1932 – again the earliest drawings are from May 1931. It was certainly completed before the winter of 1934–5, when Dr King complained that the roof leaked.[7] The design, daringly modern for 1930s Edinburgh, was a continental looking white cubic building of the type that was beginning to appear in Britain. Some derided these as 'Steamboat style' because they looked rather nautical, like a ship's bridge.

King's house was essentially single-storey, although a partial upper floor contained a guest bedroom. This gave way to an open sleeping terrace over the bow-fronted living room. Load-bearing corner windows added to the startling effect. Continental houses of this style, such as the one by Hans Scharoun at the Weissenhof estate in Stuttgart, which Spence visited in 1934, were of pioneering concrete construction and open in plan. But only the roof and stairs at Lismhor were concrete and the plan was conventional, with rooms off a corridor.

The only other Kininmonth & Spence house approaching

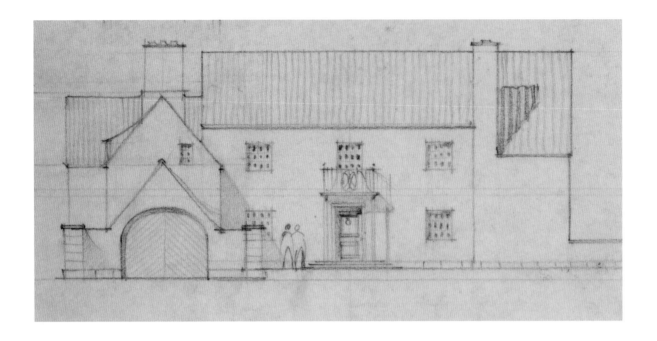

36 An unexecuted design for a house by Spence for himself, 1939
DP018479 RCAHMS

37 House at Easter Belmont, Edinburgh, for the Misses Reid, 1932
DP010912 RCAHMS

HOUSE AT EASTER BELMONT
FOR THE MISSES REID.

the modernism of the King house was Kininmonth's own [**38**].[8] He had married the painter, Caroline Sutherland, whom he had met when both were students at Edinburgh College of Art, and they managed to acquire a garden plot in an Edinburgh suburb. The consequent house, of 1933–4, was constructed in brick, but upper partitions were of wire mesh sprayed with plaster. Sliding doors to the living room allowed freer circulation. Like the King house, it had a single-storey bow-fronted living room with terrace above, but strict economy ruled out corner windows. The use of concrete was limited to the roof and the pergola, which linked the house to the garage.

The partnership received a further commission at Easter Belmont, from two sisters named Reid. A Spence perspective, dated April 1932, was exhibited at the Royal Scottish Academy the following year [**37**], while a photograph of the completed building appeared in the architectural press in 1935.[9] It was provided with a hipped roof but, like the Kininmonth and King houses, also featured a terrace on the flat roof of a bow-fronted living room.[10]

In 1934 Spence married Mary Joan Ferris, whom he had met while living in London. Until then he had lived with his

mother, Daisy, in a flat in Marchmont in Edinburgh and the change in family circumstances precipitated two designs by Spence himself, rather than as a product of the practice. The house for Daisy Spence was executed on an extremely tight budget of £900.[11] This rather colonial-looking single-storey white cottage, situated in Comiston, Edinburgh, is long and low, with Dutch gables and a tiled roof. It was perched on the edge of a steep slope, with all the rooms oriented to the south, and accessed from a corridor on the north. The interior fittings were in Arts and Crafts style and the fireplace was decorated with an arc of blue roof tiles. Basil and Joan Spence must have soon considered building a home for themselves. Indeed, there are drawings for such a house, dated 1939, which provide an interesting contrast in style with Kininmonth's *Moderne* statement [**36**].[12] The L-plan house was to be of two storeys, with a single-storey service wing containing kitchen and garage on the east, and a studio on the west. The inspiration seems to have come from Lorimer and Lutyens, yet the elevations with small-paned windows also evoke Mackintosh, as does the chimney stack rising from the ground – the latter feature being used at the Empire Exhibition [see **145**].

Kininmonth & Spence's essays in the *Moderne* style were completed with one of their few commercial buildings [**33**]. Southern Motors (1933–4), a white-rendered petrol station, on the south side of Edinburgh, with a large, glazed workshop cantilevered over the forecourt, was all the more striking by virtue of its contrast with its grey tenement neighbours. The antecedent appears to be a Robert Mallet-Stevens garage in Paris, which was illustrated in the *RIAS Journal* in 1930. However, while the French architect was pioneering construction in concrete, the Edinburgh garage employed a steel frame. The fins, which accentuated the cantilevers and gave a streamlined appearance, served no purpose other than to carry signage. These were of timber, with metal lath and cement render. Spence produced two handsome perspectives of the garage that express something of the excitement and style of the nascent motor age.

In 1934 Balfour Paul invited Kininmonth and Spence to join him in partnership. The new firm became Rowand Anderson & Paul & Partners,[13] but Paul died early in 1938 and from that point until 1946 Kininmonth and Spence were the sole partners. The merger increased the client base and brought a wider variety of work. One commercial commission gave Spence the opportunity to try out his ideas

38 Kininmonth house as published in *The Architect and Building News*, 11 October 1935
Private collection

for interior design at a prominent location for Cleghorn's, an Edinburgh manufacturer and retailer of leather goods. Cleghorn's vacated their George Street premises to make way for a new office building, Dunedin House, designed by Balfour Paul. This necessitated reconstruction of a shop for Cleghorn's in Princes Street. The drawings include a pair of colourful perspectives by Spence showing round roof lights and what appears to be a stair winding around a cylindrical core [39]. This recalls a similar motif at Leo Nachlicht's 1928 Gourmenia Restaurant in Berlin [40]. However, the Cleghorn's plans reveal that there was no cylinder or spiral and the effect was achieved with bent plywood at the back of the staircase.[14]

During this period the practice's finances were boosted by commissions for local authority housing. Although Kininmonth later regarded these as 'non-descript', the architects clearly strived to get architectural detail into their designs without incurring unacceptable costs.[15] The most interesting of these schemes was the white terrace of houses at Dunbar [41], mainly by Kininmonth, who also appears to have been responsible for houses at Burnmouth, in Berwickshire. Exhibitions and country houses such as Broughton Place, Quothquhan and Gribloch were to occupy most of Spence's time in the second half of the 1930s.

The first of these, Broughton Place, was for the Elliot family. Thomas Elliot was a medical professor in London and his wife, Martha, came from a Scottish family of industrialists. Mrs Elliot called at the Rowand Anderson & Paul & Partners offices in Rutland Square in September 1935 to discuss her requirements for a site at Broughton near Biggar, in the Scottish Borders. She wanted a romantic house in the style of Robert Lorimer, relishing the site's historical associations with the Jacobite rebel John Murray.

Spence and Kininmonth agreed to provide a pair of schemes for Mrs Elliot to choose from, quite probably aware that she had similarly instructed Joe Gleave and James Macgregor, both of whom were colleagues of Spence at Edinburgh College of Art.[16] A rapid study of Lorimer's castles was made, Kininmonth drafting a design based on Kellie Castle [42], which was visited especially. But Spence was chosen as architect on the basis of a scheme inspired by Formakin, Balmanno, and Dunderave – the former house was designed by Lorimer, the other two are castles that he restored. Spence's design for Broughton Place emulated the organic growth of a medieval tower house extended in the seventeen century and with late nineteenth-century interventions [44]. The picturesque composition was a cluster of crowstep gables, round towers, and triangular pediments,

41 Design for fishermen's housing at Dunbar, East Lothian, showing two phases of the scheme that was begun in 1934, 1950
Private collection

39 Design for Cleghorn's Shop, 129 Princes Street, Edinburgh
SC357574 RCAHMS

40 The Gourmenia Restaurant by Leo Nachlicht, Berlin, as published in *Architectural Review*, 1930
SC1054165 RCAHMS

and was the subject of considerable dialogue and much redrafting before the design was finalised. The biggest economy was in choosing brick over stone, representing a saving of £900, despite advice to the contrary by the practice.[17]

The result was perhaps more Mackintosh than Lorimer, due to the elongated fenestration, round tower and the unifying roughcast render, but it was certainly the outcome of Arts and Crafts-inspired sensibilities. The interiors have examples of 'Old Scots' wrought ironwork, reproduction Renaissance plasterwork and high-quality architectural woodwork. Spence brought in Hew Lorimer, who carved tympanums, an intricate marriage panel, another panel illustrating a Celtic fairytale, and a pair of reclining lions mounted on the gate piers.

The design process for Quothquhan in Lanarkshire was far more straightforward. Alexander Erskine-Hill, Conservative MP for North Edinburgh, instructed Spence in February 1937. He immediately visited the site and by April was able to submit plans for local authority approval. The Erskine-Hills knew precisely what they wanted. This was a copy of the nearby Culter House, which they had previously rented [43].

Quothquhan was intended as a hunting lodge and, like Broughton Place, it is of harled brick with slate roofs, but it is a different sort of Scottish fantasy. Its antecedent, Culter, is a laird's house in the form of a classical box, with rather extensive wings. Using somewhat different proportions, Spence delivered a fairly close approximation, although it displayed

a wider 1930s enthusiasm for Regency architecture. Few would mistake it for anything other than a twentieth-century building, because of its proportions and unusual, if functional, placement of chimney stacks. Nevertheless, it acknowledged its heritage by means of modest ceiling heights, slate roofs and carved scrolled skewputts [45].

In 1939 Spence wrote an article, 'Tradition in Scottish Architecture'. The background to this was the contemporary movement for cultural nationalism, itself a response to the economic recession of the late 1920s and early 1930s and a perceived loss of Scottish identity. This lobby had political, literary and social elements, some of which criticised as un-Scottish the modern style of the 1938 Empire Exhibition, with which Spence was deeply involved. Spence argued that architecture must respond to the conditions and requirements of modernity, using contemporary methods of construction and materials. This was despite his two recently completed historicist mansions; but of course the style of these had been dictated by his clients, and so Spence had to find a subsequent carefully balanced conceptual position. He concluded that traditional architecture had operated in precisely the same way as the modern functionalists:

One is led to believe that Tradition is really, firstly, a thorough appreciation of the problem without violating the materials, and using economic methods of construction. To use old forms for sentimental reasons would seem to be wrong, though an old form which would be economic and practical could be used if there was no aesthetic reason against its use.[18]

42 Kellie Castle, Fife,
a source for Broughton Place
SC802295 RCAHMS

43 Culter House, Lanarkshire,
a source for Quothquhan
SC1072396 RCAHMS

44 Broughton Place in the
Scottish Borders
SC684959 RCAHMS

Gribloch, the final in the trio of country houses, was for the industrialist John Colville, a cousin of Mrs Erskine-Hill. The site was on the edge of a moor in Stirlingshire, with commanding views to the Grampian hills. As with Broughton Place, there was a protracted dialogue between architect and clients and, despite their enormous wealth, the Colvilles were constantly demanding economies. The brief was also similar to that of the other two houses; all the facilities of the traditional country house: guest rooms, gun room, game store, servants' accommodation and so on. Again, sun and view were to determine the plan's position of the public rooms and main bedrooms, but in contrast to Broughton Place and Quothquhan, this house was to be modern in appearance [47].

By early August 1937 a scheme was sent to the clients showing a building of two storeys in an L-plan arrangement around an entrance court, with the main house on the south and the service wing to the east [46]. This did not meet the client's approval so Spence proposed further schemes,

modifying the plan to address the issues of sunlight and views. The circular hall, particularly desired by Mrs Colville, was retained, as was the bow-fronted living room with master bedroom above. This was given a balcony, but on the other terraces on the south these were omitted. This scheme formed the essence of the final design, but there was further work to be done; Mrs Colville referred to a number of country houses she admired, including one modern example, Joldwynds, 1933, in Surrey, designed by Oliver Hill, which had a convex south façade, glazed circular stair-tower and a flat roof. The new Gribloch scheme retained the copper roof of its predecessors, but with a lowered pitch. Spence's revisions still failed to completely satisfy the Colvilles, who felt progress was hampered because Spence was not devoting enough time to the project, so they consulted another architect, Perry Duncan, of New York, who liased with the clients and Spence by post. Duncan revised the design by splaying the wings further, flattening the bowed stair window into an elliptical plan, and altering the dining room so that the

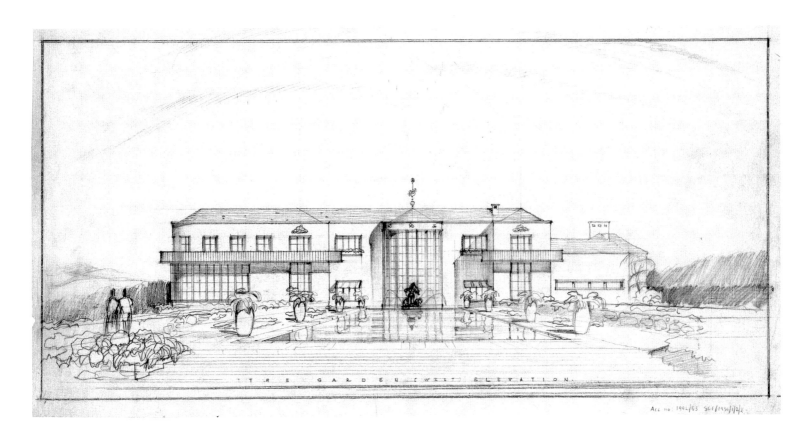

THE GARDEN (WEST) ELEVATION.

circular hall disappeared. Spence incorporated these suggestions into the scheme, amending the hall to an oval, and construction finally began in June 1938 [**48**].[19]

The original commission included a garage block and a gatekeeper's lodge. John Colville felt that the cost of the lodge was excessive and hired another architect to produce a bungalow, with art deco details that would not look out of place in most 1930s suburbs.[20] Spence's garage block, which was semi-circular with single-bay bowed pavilions, was a purer geometric expression of architectural form than the house itself. The upper storey, containing staff

accommodation, was a C-plan. The garage beneath this was lit by portholes on the façade and roof lights in the single-storey part. The car spaces, numerous enough for the vehicles of a shooting party, were arranged fan-like around the perimeter.

Spence produced designs for the interior of the house but the clients also brought in other consultants and made contributions themselves. John Colville, for instance, designed wrought-iron window grilles, which Spence disliked. John Hill, of the London interior design company Green & Abbott, designed fireplaces, door surrounds and other

48 The oval staircase hall at Gribloch as published in *Country Life*, 12 January 1951
Country Life

various details and advised on furniture, fittings and colour. The resulting interiors, which were published in *Country Life* in 1951, have some traditional architectural features, such as rope mouldings and arched doorways. These, together with art deco furniture and details, helped to create the blend of *Moderne* and Regency, often described as 'Hollywood', to which the clients aspired.

When the Colvilles eventually moved into Gribloch in December 1939, Spence had been called to active duty, leaving Kininmonth to deal with the final stages of this and other outstanding commissions. These included Spence's first school, Kilsyth Academy [**49**], which had reached first floor level when abandoned in July 1940 (it was completed to an enlarged design after the war). Instigated by the Scottish Committee of the Council for Arts and Industry as the Scottish School for Art and Industry, it was a progressive new teaching environment aimed at improving the quality of the nation's industrial output through education of the work force. Given his three country houses and the Empire Exhibition, it is remarkable that Spence found time for the ten months of research that went into its planning. A prominent hilltop site was chosen, allowing acres of playing fields around the layout of low buildings interconnected by spinal corridors. Innovations included a glass gable to the gymnasium, made possible by the use of reinforced concrete, and a swimming pool, a wall of which could be opened up in fine weather. Further features included a clock tower (for which Thomas Whalen produced a relief sculpture) and a bowed

glass-fronted stair tower. The external rendering contained quartz and granite chips that would glisten in the sun.

Thus ended the first phase of Basil Spence's career; eight years in practice in which he became firmly established as a prominent Scottish architect, with experience in almost every field of architecture. After the Second World War, his drive and ambition were undiminished and his sphere of operations spanned the length and breadth of Britain and beyond.

49 Design model for Kilsyth Academy, Kilsyth, late 1930s
SC944145 RCAHMS

EXHIBITION DESIGN

BRIAN EDWARDS

The architectural style of Basil Spence was well suited to that of the design of exhibition stands. His light and elegant approach, particularly in the years before and after World War Two, proved attractive to those clients who wanted, through the design of exhibition pavilions, to project a popular and progressive image. In many ways Spence used exhibition architecture to test and develop ideas which later found expression in more permanent works, and in the process allowed himself to adopt the kind of free-wheeling approach employed not by trained architects but by industrial designers. Writing in 1950 Spence said that 'exhibitions are fundamentally the forcing house for experiments which will … take on more solid form at some later date'.[1] These experiments at first involved lightweight construction, new materials and decorative effects, while later exhibition projects showed a testing of sculptural forms and abstract composition.

Spence's perspective sketches could quickly evoke the spirit of a design, attractive to both those paying for the exhibition stand and those given the task of its production. These drawings were light, gay and colourful, sometimes lit dramatically, but always populated by people set sparingly against the background of materials on display. Spence had an undoubted flair for such design although he did worry that his success in this arena would lead to him being branded the designer of temporary pavilions rather than an architect of buildings of greater substance. However, as he noted, the temporary nature of exhibitions and the reality of stands normally existing inside other structures, gave the architect the chance to enjoy 'adventures into engineering theory'.[2] What he meant by this was the excitement of applying innovative structural solutions and dynamic form.

In 1934 Basil Spence designed his first exhibition pavilion at the age of only twenty-seven. It was for the Edinburgh Architectural Association and consisted of a stand displaying modern design and construction methods housed at the Waverley Exhibition Centre in Edinburgh. Two years later, he was the designer of an exhibition at the Royal Scottish Museum on Scottish Everyday Art.[3] This quickly led to his appointment to design the more ambitious pavilion for the Scottish Development Council at the Johannesburg Empire Exhibition of 1936. These exhibition pavilions drew Spence to the attention of Thomas Tait, who invited him to join the design team for the Empire Exhibition staged in Glasgow's Bellahouston Park two years later. Tait admired Spence's distinctive blend of Scandinavian modernism and Scottish romanticism, which was fashionable amongst younger architects in Edinburgh. Tait also liked Spence's flair and personality, believing it suited this type of work, which relied upon its popular appeal.

What Spence brought to the design of these pre-war exhibitions was a certain theatricality which lightened spirits dampened by recession in the industrial heartlands of Scotland. The young architect was a keen advocate of contemporary construction methods (such as aluminium framing) and the use of new materials made available as a result of innovations in the chemical industry. Although these materials would not have survived the harsh climate of Scotland, exhibition pavilions provided the opportunity to place new design approaches before the public, either in a sheltered indoor world or during a brief outdoor summer. Since government-sponsored exhibitions were largely propagandist in nature, the cheerful yet sophisticated designs of Spence helped educate both public and consumers alike.

Although few details survive of Spence's design for the Johannesburg exhibition, it appears to have been similar to the Scottish Pavilion designed by Spence at the Empire Exhibition held in Glasgow in 1938 [51]. Here the Scandinavian influence is most marked, with bands of curved windows set into sleek white walls reminiscent of contemporary practice in Stockholm. Slender towers topped with radio masts and flagpoles added to the effect, as did touches of blue paint. At the time Spence acknowledged the collaboration of Thomas Tait in the design but it was widely understood as primarily Spence's conception. As co-ordinating architect for the Empire Exhibition, Tait probably had some influence on massing but little more. Significantly, Tait was instrumental in sending Spence to the

50 Design for the Enterprise Scotland exhibition at the Royal Museum of Scotland, Edinburgh, 1947
DP012247 RCAHMS

Paris International Exhibition in June 1937 where he would have seen Picasso's mural *Guernica* in the Spanish Pavilion (surely an inspiration for later artist / architect collaboration) as well as Alvar Aalto's seminal Finnish Pavilion. Spence also designed the Council for Art and Industry Pavilion in the form of an ideal house for the Scottish countryside [see **145**]. Although the design was markedly traditional with a pitched roof and pronounced chimney stack, it was furnished with the latest in contemporary fittings. Compared with housing exhibitions in Europe at the time, distinguished by the widespread use of flat roofs, horizontal balconies and sun terraces, the design by Spence was reserved but reflected the lingering taste in Scotland for traditional architecture, particularly in rural areas.

In parallel with these public commissions Spence was involved in designing trade stands for a number of major manufacturing companies, most based in the west of Scotland but some further afield. A notable early example was the ICI Pavilion, again for the Empire Exhibition, which featured three interlocking curved towers joined by shiny cupro-nickel tubes (a new material developed by the company) lit with coloured lights to evoke something of the spirit of modern industry [**52**]. The approach was perhaps more Odeonesque than Russian Constructivism but the vertical emphasis and sculptural modelling resulted in an external profile which stood out amongst the other pavilions. Spence

51 The Empire Exhibition, Glasgow, 1938
SC1072397 RCAHMS

52 The ICI Pavilion at night, Empire Exhibition, Glasgow, 1938
SC560039 RCAHMS

had won the commission in a limited competition, again on Tait's recommendation, no doubt using his fluency of drawing and enthusiasm to good effect.[4] However, it was a design given some thought: each tower formed part of a circle in plan and represented the raw materials of the chemical industry – earth, air and water – allowing the architect to employ metaphor as well as function to generate the overall conception. The construction of the lofty towers also gave Spence the opportunity to show off ICI's new plastics and finishes.[5] He was keen to ensure that the values of the company, as well as its products, balanced the universal ideals of modernism. Robert Hurd, a major architect of the Scottish 1930s, described the ICI Pavilion as the best at the Empire Exhibition.[6]

In these pre-war designs Spence sought where possible to employ artists to add lustre and interest to his architectural ideas. Abstract murals, free-standing sculpture and friezes were incorporated into the overall framework under Spence's direction. Invariably Spence nominated artists he had known at Edinburgh College of Art – either fellow students or members of the teaching staff. Thus he commissioned Thomas Whalen to provide a series of semi-abstract sculptural panels to embellish the pylons of the ICI Pavilion, and Archibald Dawson to fashion a free-standing figure of St Andrew in the Scottish Pavilion. The artist Walter Pritchard also provided a large painting titled *Order and Chaos*, which in some ways anticipated forthcoming conflicts.

Compared with the immediate post-war years, money from government and industry, coupled with a ready supply of construction materials, provided Spence with the chance to experiment away from the more conservative arena of mainstream architectural practice in Edinburgh. Such work was also quite well paid, with Spence earning much the same design fee for the Scottish pavilion at Johannesburg as that for Quothquhan [see **45**], a large country house then on the drawing board.[7] But the main benefit for the young architect was the exposure to new ideas and methods of working which this type of design provided. In turn, the name Basil Spence and his perspective drawings were finding their way into newspapers and reviews in magazines such as *Homes and Gardens*. This helped ensure patronage after the war.

Writing a chapter in Misha Black's book *Exhibition Design* published in 1950, Spence observed that exhibitions were 'pure design' with the best effects achieved by lightweight materials and prefabrication.[8] Building on

earlier experience, Spence's pavilions after the war made particular use of tubular aluminium framing, plywood box girders and steel cables, often sheathing the construction in fabrics of various colours or the new plastics coming onto the market. This is most evident in the Council of Industrial Design's 1947 exhibition, Enterprise Scotland. Housed in the Royal Scottish Museum in Edinburgh, it consisted of a number of cone-shaped towers lit from above and draped in colourful translucent cloth [**50**]. Each tower surmounted an exhibit of modern Scottish products, from shoes to toys and glass. Although an unabashed promotion of contemporary Scottish design within the grandiose setting of a monumental nineteenth-century museum, Spence, working with the designer James Gardner, managed to achieve an effect that was theatrical and appropriately light-hearted.[9]

Exhibition architecture provided Spence with the opportunity to employ materials developed as part of the war effort, such as plywood, perspex and aerocrete (a form of thin but strong concrete). The use of such relatively new materials suited the industrial themes of post-war exhibitions such as Britain Can Make It, held in London in 1946 [**53**], and the Scottish Industries Exhibition of 1949 held in Kelvin Hall, Glasgow [**54**]. At the latter, Spence designed a number of stands, including one for Babcock and Wilcox, a major manufacturer for the power industry. Spence suspended a wing-like ceiling from a space frame, freeing the area below to display the company's pumps and turbines. At the Scottish Council (Development and Industry) stand a more traditional image was created with the help of semi-abstract heraldic shields (by Walter Pritchard) set on a curved screen of spun glass.[10] At the Council for Industrial Design stand there was a revolving cone set on a point displaying examples of modern design surrounded by panels suspended from above [**56**]. By way of contrast, for the furniture manufacturer H. Morris and Co., Ltd, Spence designed a stand with textured walls, evoking a more traditional Scottish mood [**55**]. Against the rough walls he placed the modern furniture designs of the company (chairs, low table and sideboard), some of which included the elegant Allegro range made of laminated wood and designed by Spence (examples of which are now in the collection of the Museum of Modern Art in New York). Spence also commissioned the artist John Hutton (with whom he would subsequently work at Coventry Cathedral) to design an abstract mural based upon the lamination of wood employed in the furniture manufactured by Morris.[11]

53 Design for the Hall of the Future at the Britain Can Make It exhibition, 1946
DP005339 RCAHMS

As with his pre-war exhibition experience, Spence moved effortlessly between public and private commissions. Amongst his many private clients were the airline companies BEA and BOAC, the thread manufacturer J. and P. Coates Ltd, the carpet maker Templeton's, the department store Wylie and Lochead [57], and further work flowed from ICI. Since many of his clients moved their trade stands from one location to another (such as ICI, for whom Spence designed stands for exhibitions in Glasgow, London, Shrewsbury and Copenhagen) he employed designs where elements could be readily dismantled, shipped and re-erected. This was needed not only to save money but because a licence was required to buy construction materials up to 1952.

The demands of prefabrication, coupled with the availability of new materials, provided the means to create dramatic effects at little cost. This was nowhere more evident than in the slightly earlier Chemistry at your Service exhibition held in London in 1946. Here Spence, acting as co-ordinating architect, employed colourful PVC sheets, felt and painted lino to create a swirling diagrammatic impression of molecular chemistry.[12] In this one suspects that Spence's experience as a camouflage officer in the war, where big effects at low cost were imperative, played their part.

In his various exhibition designs preceding the Festival of Britain in 1951 Spence sought a modern, elegant and somewhat theatrical effect. His stands looked good not only when published in journals and newspapers, but also in the trade literature of the companies involved. Such photographs, coupled with the publication of a number of his perspective drawings in the architectural press, helped project an image of an imaginative, versatile and still youthful architect. The contribution made by Spence to post-war exhibition architecture, particularly the influential Britain Can Make It exhibition held in London, led to the award of an OBE in 1948.

In these years, architectural commissions were thin on the ground. Spence, together with dynamic contemporaries such as Hugh Casson,[13] were more fully employed in the design of exhibition pavilions than with permanent architecture. Thus it seems reasonable to conclude that exhibition design had a lasting effect on Spence, not least on the major projects which he undertook in the 1950s, such as Coventry Cathedral. Exhibition design had allowed Spence to collaborate with artists, to explore new structural methods and materials, and to develop a popular architecture based upon largely visual effects. It had also encouraged Spence to see

himself as a co-ordinator of the efforts of others; an essential quality in his role of master-plan designer of Britain Can Make It. In this capacity Spence nurtured talent within his own office and the wider design and artistic community. It had also helped him develop his talent for public speaking, using terms which were free of jargon yet carried conviction.

Spence had moved from an architecture of largely white structures of painted plaster on a wooden or steel frame in the 1930s to more dramatic effects of light and colour in the 1940s. The earlier influence of the 1930 Stockholm Exhibition and the 1937 Paris Exhibition (which involved designers working closely with artists of the stature of Pablo Picasso) led Spence to embellish his exhibition designs with murals, banners or decorative panels. By the 1950s Spence began to employ the full repertoire of architectural and constructivist possibilities, and nowhere is this more apparent than in his designs for the Festival of Britain of 1951, where he was responsible for three interconnected structures: the Sea and Ships Pavilion [**58**], Nelson Pier and the Skylark Restaurant. They formed an important group between the Dome of Discovery by Ralph Tubbs and the River Thames.

Spence was approached by Hugh Casson in 1950, the two having first met twelve years earlier at the Glasgow Empire Exhibition, which Casson was then reviewing for the *Architectural Review*.[14] Casson, like Spence, was an architect for whom visual appeal mattered as much as function, and had been appointed as co-ordinating architect for the Festival of Britain a few months earlier. The site facing the Thames on the South Bank was to include about thirty pavilions, with some buildings such as the Royal Festival Hall (designed by Spence's Edinburgh College of Art friend and rival, Robert Matthew, together with Leslie Martin) remaining after the festival as part of the site's permanent regeneration.

The design by Spence for the Sea and Ships Pavilion developed from earlier ideas such as the BOAC and BEA stands, with their use of the cutaway aircraft fuselages into which the public could go. Spence also re-employed the dramatic effects of exaggerated height and atmosphere utilised in the 1938 ICI Pavilion as well as the Babcock and Wilcox stand at the Scottish Industries Exhibition of 1949 with its suspended ceiling hung from an exposed steel framework. There was no hint of separation between what was to be displayed and the architectural framework – in fact both were smoothly and dramatically united within the pavilion.

The Sea and Ships Pavilion was intended to celebrate

the fact that Britain was a maritime nation, and the building was to house a number of models of ocean-going liners as well as diesel turbines and other nautical displays, many with their origins in the Scottish Clydeside story. In effect, the pavilion was to be more shipyard than conventional building, with the ships themselves cut theatrically in section and suspended from the roof. Another legacy of earlier ideas was the verticality of form, dramatically emphasised from above by light entering from on high. The building was long in plan, placed parallel to the Embankment and with elements of the exhibition projecting outwards through the walls. A giant framework of steel towers and gantries tied the composition together. The overall effect was more deconstruction than construction, Spence capturing the spirit of a modern shipyard scene with its essays in incompleteness [**6, 59**].

A particular type of architect was required for the design of exhibition pavilions: someone able to draw well, visualise quickly, speak lucidly about the role of design in providing a progressive image, and modest enough to accept the limitations of budget and impermanence. Spence was such an architect and preferred this type of work to the other major stream of post-war practice, namely building repairs and restoration. One benefit which Spence acknowledged, following success in the Coventry Cathedral competition in 1951, was the way exhibition design had kept him in the public eye. However, architects who spend too much time in the artificial world of exhibitions run the risk of employing structure, light and interior space in too decorative or trivial a manner. The lack of gravitas in such work arguably found its way into some of the projects which passed through Spence's hands in the decade after the war. For example, some of the effects at Coventry Cathedral hint at the design of exhibition pavilions rather than that of ecclesiastical architecture.

The last exhibition building designed by Spence was his largest and arguably most controversial project. It was the British Pavilion at Expo '67, one of seventy-seven national pavilions at the world exposition housed in Montreal over the summer of 1967 [**60**]. The uniting theme of the Expo was the humanist one of 'Man and his World', and the site chosen was the island of Notre Dame in the St Lawrence River. Expo '67 became a showpiece of contemporary architecture, public sculpture, landscape design and new modes of urban transport. To this Spence made his own distinctive contribution. The attention Expo '67 enjoyed in

56 Design for the Council for Industrial Design stand at the Scottish Industries Exhibition, Kelvin Hall, Glasgow, 1949
DP010911 RCAHMS

57 Design for the Wylie and Lochead exhibition stand at the Scottish Industries Exhibition, Kelvin Hall, Glasgow, 1949
DP010877 RCAHMS

opposite

58 Design for the Sea and Ships Pavilion, Festival of Britain, London, 1951
DP026863 RCAHMS

59 Sea and Ships Pavilion, Festival of Britain, London, 1951
Private collection

popular and professional journals encouraged commentators at the time to call it the most successful world fair of the twentieth century.[15] Although it was widely seen as one of the great flowerings of modernism in a city noted for bold contemporary urbanism, a closer examination suggests that the ambiguities of postmodernism were also present. In this, Spence played an important role.

Within the general theme of 'Man and his World', nations were expected to 'demonstrate the wealth of our common knowledge and emphasise the youth of the world, the legacy of the past and the prospect of things to come'.[16] This framework encouraged the British Government to decide on the specific themes for the exhibitions to be contained within the pavilion, each of which was to be developed by a different designer under Spence's overall control. The themes and designers were:

The Shaping of the Nation by Sean Kenny
The Genius of Britain by Beverley Pick
Britain Today by James Gardner
Industrial Britain by Theo Crosby
Britain in the World by Mario Armengol

Since Spence knew the designers in question and had advised on their appointment (Kenny, Gardner and Armengol through their participation in the Festival of Britain in 1951, and Crosby and Pick via the Royal Academy, London, where Spence held the largely honorary position of Professor of Architecture) his task of co-ordination did not prove difficult.

Inspired perhaps by the implied modernity and sense of nationhood of the five themes, Spence pronounced within a year of his appointment that he had produced a 'craggy, tough and uncompromising design ... using large forms with an industrial bias'.[17] However, the pavilion was not to be an abstract design devoid of cultural reference but one where, in deference to the British being an island people (as Spence put it), the mass of the pavilion was to rise out of the water. This mass, in fact, consisted of five connected architectural elements each intended to house one of the designated themes. To seek the right contemporary flavour Spence said that there should be no 'flags or bunting, grass or flowers', suggesting he saw the design as needing to be robust and gritty in flavour.[18]

It is clear from the earliest pencil sketches that Spence sought an uncompromisingly modern design but one which, with its dynamic shapes, was also 'artistic' in spirit. The pavilion had, he said, to be able to be perceived as a unified container for the five themed exhibits whilst also producing a distinct experience as a whole.[19] Spence deliberately avoided the effect of openness favoured by other pavilion architects, notably Frei Otto at the German Pavilion and Buckminster Fuller at the USA Pavilion. He wanted 'a massive piece of sculpture, with a big strong silhouette' containing a large interior space away from the 'heat and sun where the eye can take a rest from the glare'.[20] Elaborating on his views in October 1965 to students at McGill University, Spence referred to himself as a humanist architect creating buildings which were enriching and comfortable places for people to live in.[21] He went on to explain that exhibition architecture was something completely different in nature from the design of ordinary buildings because of their role as a crucible for experimentation and a vehicle for national propaganda. In describing his design as 'compelling and vital ... and an eye catcher from any angle',[22] Spence seemed to be suggesting that he was aware of the limitations of mainstream modernism in providing a pavilion design which embodied the requisite combination of startling form and cultural metaphor. He was already looking to art to provide the answer.

The pavilion, with its asymmetrical tower and surrounding reflective pools, was planned around three sides of a broad square nearly three acres in area [62]. The fourth side was equipped with an elevated deck overlooking a lagoon, which in turn led via grand flights of steps to the entrance, marked by a fountain. Once inside the pavilion the separate exhibition halls were linked at various levels to a lighthouse-like tower by covered walkways, ramps and escalators. The overall effect, according to Spence, was that of 'an island on an island site to represent the basic idea of Britain'.[23] Here Spence appears to be departing from his earlier exhibition design practice where the emphasis was upon openness, preferring instead to encapsulate architecturally the insular nature of the British people. In fact, the Expo site with its broad rivers inspired Spence to create a building that would rise like 'the white cliffs of Dover'.[24]

One element which changed from the initial designs was that of the tower. Spence in his early proposals had sought to combine tower and base in one sweeping structure but, as the design developed, the tower became more of a separate building. Spence, encouraged by comments from the Central Office of Information (COI) that they wanted to house a Whittle jet engine somewhere in the pavilion, designed a tower that would rise above the rooftops of the other pavilions. By 1966 the tower had become the focus of the theme 'Industrial Britain', designed around the subjects of transport and power. The Whittle engine was to be suspended in the tower beneath roof lights and viewed by visitors from underneath. Spence had frequently used the tower motif in his earlier exhibition designs; in each case the tower could be entered into, with the perception of height counter-balancing the low volumes of the main exhibition spaces. He applied the same effect at Expo.

As built, the solidity of the British Pavilion and irregular shape of the tower attracted wide comment and some rude humour. It was subsequently interpreted by James Callaghan, then the Chancellor of the Exchequer, as 'looking like Eddystone Lighthouse seen from Plymouth Hoe',[25] whilst the correspondent for *Le Petit Journal* likened the pavilion to the Rock of Gibraltar.[26] He was already looking to art to provide the answer anticipating, perhaps, the ideas of Frank Gehry. It certainly stood in marked contrast to most other pavilions, which were largely symmetrical structures with much angled glazing. Spence had designed the British Pavilion to be lit by roof lights from above, creating dramatic

60 Model for the British
Pavilion at Expo '67, Montreal
SC1047272 RCAHMS

61 Sketch design for the
British Pavilion at Expo '67,
Montreal, 1965
SC956946 RCAHMS

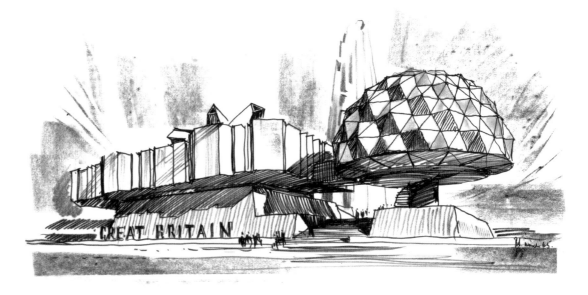

62 British Pavilion at Expo '67, Montreal
Private collection

63 Detail of the British Pavilion at Expo '67, Montreal, with Henry Moore's sculpture *Locking Piece*
SC1047362 RCAHMS

64 Interior of the British Pavilion at Expo '67, Montreal. Astrid Zydower with the figures she sculpted for the 'Britain Today' section designed by James Gardner.
SC1047356 RCAHMS

effects of natural and artificial light. These roof windows were tucked behind parapets, adding to the severity of the design. The walls, in white asbestos cement sheets, rose like cliffs of chalk as the architect had intended. The image was one of Britain secure within its fortress of white cladding, yet inside there was a world of high technology, glamour and popular culture. This ambivalence between exterior form and interior content worried architectural commentators but generally appealed to the public at large.

Expo '67 exposed the tension between a universal ideal and the romantic searching for national identity in modern exhibition design. The British Pavilion was rich in drama and ambiguity, with Spence perhaps anticipating the wider disenchantment at a world dominated by globalisation and technology. Looking back over the many exhibition designs undertaken by Spence between 1934 and 1967, it becomes evident that there is more experimentation in this work than in his more orthodox architectural output. However, just as the Barcelona Pavilion contained the germ of ideas which Mies van der Rohe developed more fully in later projects,[27] so too with the pavilions designed by Spence.

His experiments in architectural space, construction, colour and promenade found their way into the building projects of the 1950s and 1960s. (This is evident in the design of Coventry Cathedral and in some of the early schemes for the University of Sussex.) Arguably too, some of the variations produced for the British Pavilion at Expo '67 point towards the compositional arrangement of the Parliament Building in New Zealand. Likewise the angled silhouette of the Expo tower hints at the treatment at the top of the Hyde Park Barracks [97]. It is clear that Spence used exhibition design not just to test ideas but to push forward the frontiers of his own architectural practice and perhaps of others as well.

SHAPING THE SACRED
SPENCE AS CHURCH-BUILDER
LOUISE CAMPBELL

Coventry Cathedral, the premier building of Britain's post-war reconstruction, transformed the career of its architect. Between the announcement in August 1951 that he had won the competition to design a new cathedral, and the consecration of the completed building in May 1962, Basil Spence achieved the pinnacle of professional recognition: he was elected President of the RIBA in 1958, knighted in 1960, elected Royal Academician in 1960, and appointed Professor of Architecture at the Royal Academy in 1961. Still more significant was the way in which Coventry re-configured Spence's practice. He established a permanent office in London, recruited new staff and identified the key individuals and firms whose expertise eased Spence's assimilation into the English building world.

Meanwhile, that world itself stood poised on the cusp of change. After the war, church design was regarded as the realm of the specialist; but with the lifting of restrictions on building in 1954, a generation of designers who had been waiting for opportunities to build launched themselves into practice. By 1958, church design was drawn inexorably into the lively critical debates which accompanied economic recovery and the expansion of the architectural profession. At the end of the decade, a new crop of churches appeared which were informed by a close analysis of the relationship between church functions and church architecture. The new cathedral, whose construction spanned this period of rapid change, apparently 'walked right into this debate' about the ideal form of the space of worship.[1]

These changes meant that Spence's victory in the 1951 competition had unforeseen consequences. By virtue of his work on the cathedral, Spence became a household name, regarded in the eyes of the public as a glamorous moderniser. By the same token, however, as architect of the building which represented Britain's recovery, Spence came to be identified as an establishment figure. In the 1960s, a decade characterised by its irreverent attitudes to authority, Spence's work for church and government exposed him to the unforgiving gaze of an aggressive avant-garde.

Spence's fame as architect of the cathedral also served

to eclipse his achievement as designer of eleven parish churches in England and Scotland, a crematorium and a non-denominational university chapel. The symbolic and ceremonial functions of the new cathedral militated against innovation; elsewhere, however, Spence was freer to explore new spatial concepts and to develop his use of light to create a series of powerful and highly personal buildings.

In 1955 – as the foundations of the new cathedral were being prepared – Spence wrote: 'I have not tried to make an exciting building … a cathedral should not arouse excitement, but a deep emotion, and it must express the canons of the Christian faith'.[2] This statement provides the key to a design which had a profound resonance for post-war visitors. In 1951, the Festival of Britain allowed a glimpse of the future beyond austerity: a world of light, modernity and fun. Coventry Cathedral represented a serious counterpart to these celebrations, in the shape of a traditional building type, designed for worship and permanence.[3] In contrast to the way in which the Festival of Britain created a lightweight counterfoil to the ponderous Victorian buildings lining the north bank of the River Thames, the new cathedral functioned as a vital conduit to the past, both the tangible past of a Midlands city shaped by powerful guilds and modern industries, and vaguer concepts of the past symbolised by Gothic architecture and the established church. For Britons experiencing an uncomfortable present and an uncertain future, the project offered a powerful sheet-anchor.[4] Spence's design commemorated the human and architectural losses of the air raid on Coventry in 1940 by retaining the roofless ruins of the medieval cathedral of St Michael [66] in their entirety, together with the makeshift altar of shattered stones which had been set up in its sanctuary in the aftermath of the blitz.[5]

These paved ruins served as a memorial garden and a forecourt to the new cathedral, to which it was connected by a columned porch [67, 68]. The new cathedral was designed as a continuum of the old in terms of its sandstone walling, the proportions of its carefully spaced bays, and the placing of choir and altar at the head of a long nave. Features

65 Coventry Cathedral, the Chapel of Industry, 1962. Carved inscription by Ralph Beyer, candleholders by Hans Coper, suspended crown of thorns by Geoffrey Clarke.
SC1029709 RCAHMS

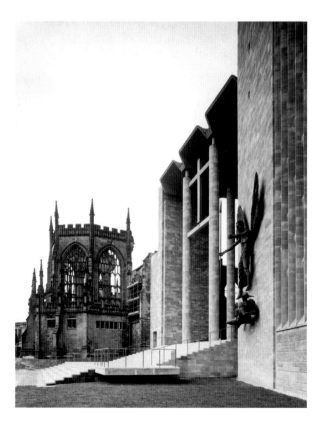

like angled nave recesses (reminiscent of side-chapels), a Chapter House, a ceiling vault, stained glass, tapestry and carved clergy stalls served not just to echo elements of the old cathedral but to provide rich opportunities for design and craftmanship [**69**]. This design, while fostering vibrant new traditions of glass and carving, also promised to contribute to the renewal of a national architecture. Spence's design had powerful support. In 1952 the President of the RIBA (who was one of the assessors of the Coventry competition) stressed the importance of sustaining the art of architecture in an age of austerity by erecting 'a few really fine quality buildings' and encouraging a renaissance of regional arts and crafts.[6] Two years later, the Minister of Works in the first post-war Conservative Government granted permission for work to begin on the cathedral in the following terms: 'The Cathedral is not a building which concerns Coventry … alone … We cannot tell how many people are waiting in this country and abroad for this church to rise and prove that English traditions live again after the blitz.'[7] Spence steered a diplomatic course between the different aspirations of the city (whose architect was struggling for resources to rebuild it), the burgeoning architectural profession, and those who regarded the new cathedral as a potent emblem of national regeneration.

66 Coventry Cathedral, view from the west of the ruined interior, 1940
SC1029513 RCAHMS

67 Coventry Cathedral from the ruins of the old cathedral
SC1071284 RCAHMS

68 Coventry Cathedral, main approach from Priory Street
SC1066470 RCAHMS

opposite

69 Coventry Cathedral, view towards the altar
SC1066474 RCAHMS

Still trickier were Spence's relations with the clergy. The Bishop and Provost of Coventry told competitors that the altar should provide a focus for worship and an invitation to communion. 'This should be the ideal of the architect, not to conceive a building and place in it an altar, but to conceive an altar and to create a building.'[8] Spence, subsequently encouraged by the progressive Bishop Gorton to experiment with the layout of the new cathedral, produced plans in late 1951 which made the altar seem more accessible by re-grouping the clergy and choir stalls behind and around it [72]. It was this kind of dialogue between architect and clergy which inspired much innovatory church design in the 1950s. But the decision-making process at Coventry Cathedral was complicated by being controlled by a building committee with a majority of lay members. After their veto of the revised plan, Spence was forced to revert to his original layout.[9] What was, and remained, central to Spence's design was the importance of symbolism. The meaningful and intimate relationship between clergy and congregation effected at new parish churches like St Paul's Bow Common, London in 1960 was instead evoked at Coventry by the subtle co-ordination of art and architecture.[10] A tapestry designed by Graham Sutherland to hang above the altar was originally conceived as linking the heavenly and earthly spheres [71]. Spence's early perspectives show a row of apostles at the tapestry's base, directly above the seated clergy in the revised layout, with the Bishop's throne positioned beneath the figure of the risen Christ [72]. On either side of the tapestry, figures of the saints in triumph and of angels and archangels were envisaged flanking the figure of Christ; they found a corresponding echo in the flying angels and images of the saints in their life on earth, with the emblems of their martyrdom, engraved by John Hutton on the glass screen at the entrance to the cathedral [70].

Although these details were omitted from the final tapestry, an elaborate iconography emphasised the Christian doctrines of sacrifice and resurrection, which the juxtaposition of the old and new cathedrals conveyed [68]. Visitors entering the cathedral by the main steps beside Epstein's sculpted group of St Michael and the Devil [73], passed the ghostly figures etched upon the screen, redolent of the victims of war as well as of the sculpted portals of Romanesque cathedrals, to confront the great tapestry at the head of the nave. To this their eyes were drawn via an accelerated perspective established by the gradual diminution of the intervals between nave columns, by the canted side-walls, and by the

70 The entrance screen at Coventry Cathedral, engraved by John Hutton
SC1029717 RCAHMS

71 Basil Spence, oil sketch of the interior of Coventry Cathedral, September 1951
DP004288 RCAHMS

72 Spence's revised arrangement of the chancel, November 1951, which was subsequently rejected.
Private collection

directional light which – admitted through narrow window apertures – streaked interior surfaces with colour [**74**]. The metaphorical journey from suffering to redemption was symbolised by the colour spectrum of the stained glass designed by artists from the Royal College of Art – from green near the entrance to rich reds at mid-nave to golden-white beside the altar – enhancing the effect of progress through time and space.

The clarity and forcefulness of the architectural rhetoric employed here has been identified by Caroline van Eck as something distinctive to the traditions of the Church of England, with its emphasis upon the church as auditorium, its concern with furniture – altar, font, pulpit – to convey key aspects of doctrine, and its stratagem of persuading by establishing a common ground of shared experience.[11]

The finale of the popular film *Mrs Miniver* (1942), with its rousing call to continue the fight for freedom, made from the pulpit of a bombed church, makes a comparable reference to the shared experience of war, with architecture serving as both a reminder of the tragic past and a token of survival. The character of Spence's design, while helping to link the old cathedral and the new, connecting the tradition of Anglican church-building (which the Victorian period helped identify as Gothic) and the post-war future, also had a more personal significance. The delicate decorative detailing of stonework, wood and metal in Spence's competition drawings suggest the importance of the Gothic for him as a student, and his admiration for Robert Lorimer, key architect of early twentieth-century Scotland [**75, 76**]. This Gothic character remained important in the design of the new cathedral, notably in the vaulting system, the roof (timber below and copper-clad above, covering a layer of concrete) and in the drum-shaped Chapel of Industry and Chapter House beneath it, which, flanking the buttressed north end of the cathedral, created a silhouette which was recognisably cathedral-like [**78**].

Despite modifications to the design in 1956, involving the substitution of concrete blocks – roughly rendered – for stone on the interior walls, the cathedral's residual Gothic character was accentuated by the tapering cruciform columns, the diamond vaulting composed of delicate concrete ribs supporting a canopy of timber slats, arranged in pyramids, and the design of the canopies of the choir stalls, rising in fantastic peaks above the seat of Provost and Bishop [see **140**]. Externally and internally, the cathedral design gained

in vigour in the late 1950s, as Spence refined and simplified his design. A memorandum of 1960 described the jewel-bright colours of the clergy vestments designed by John Piper in the context of the redesigned chancel: 'the movement of the clergy must be imagined against the background of austere simplicity – the black floor, the white walls, the simple wood of the choir stalls, the richness of the tapestry beyond'.[12] These devices, Spence suggested to the new Provost, offered a vital alternative to a 'cosy C. of E.' atmosphere.[13] The attention paid to the staging of the liturgy supports Van Eck's suggestion of a staged experience, a dramatisation of the emotional and physical experience of worship by the orchestration of architecture and design. It also conveys Spence's powerful visual and imaginative engagement with his design [see **136**].

73 Coventry Cathedral, detail showing Jacob Epstein's sculpture of *St Michael and the Devil* SC1029630 RCAHMS

74 Coventry Cathedral, nave recesses with stained glass by Lawrence Lee and Geoffrey Clarke and Tablets of the Word carved by Ralph Beyer SC1029688 RCAHMS

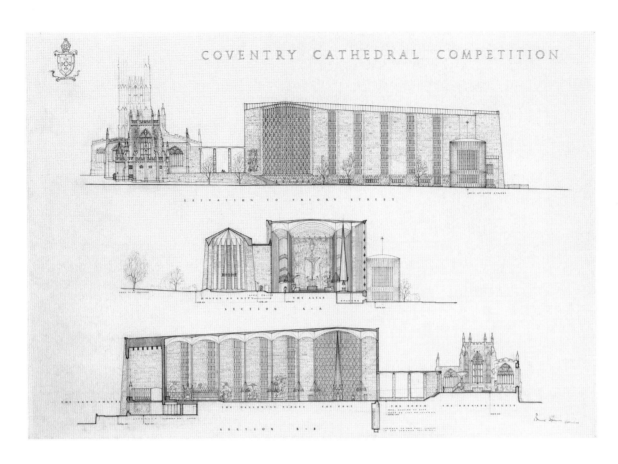

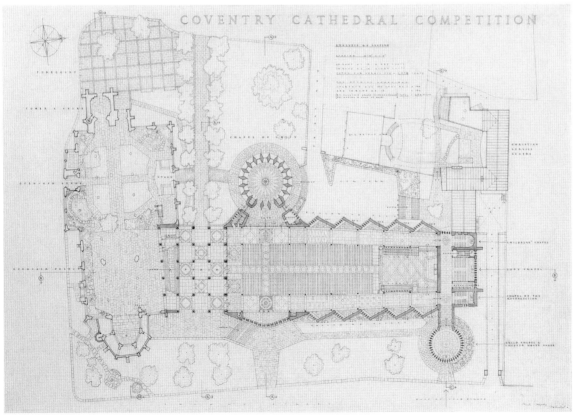

75 Coventry Cathedral competition: elevation and sections, 1951
DP028422 RCAHMS

76 Coventry Cathedral competition: plan, 1951
DP024916 RCAHMS

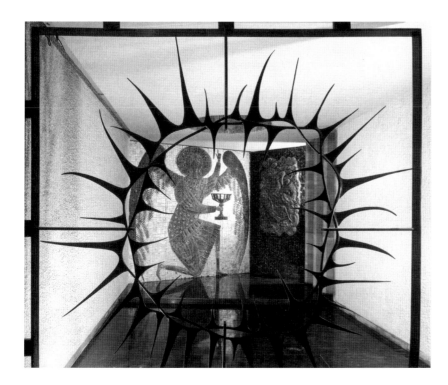

During the intense final period of work on the cathedral, Spence defended his approach against the functional imperatives on which younger church designers were beginning to insist.[14] Light was deployed to create drama and incident, and to raise the emotional temperature, as in John Piper's great baptistery window [see **138**], where – as in Bernini's design of the Cathedra Petri in St Peter's, Rome – a central burst of golden glass provided a focus which could hold its own with the architecture.[15] Elsewhere, hidden light sources illuminated dense areas of colour and decoration, as in the Gethsemane Chapel [**77**], where reflective surfaces caught the eye to the right of the Lady Chapel. Expanses of plain surface contrasted with areas of elaborate pattern; opacity and robust texture told against sparkle and sheen. While aspects of the cathedral design were rooted in the Anglican tradition, Nikolaus Pevsner attributed others to Scotland, suggesting that Coventry's design, with its zig-zag walls and rich detailing, revealed Spence's 'capacity to draw on an obscure store of Celtic fantasy and magic'.[16]

In 1956, the American historian Henry-Russell Hitchcock – in an interview where he criticised the cathedral design for its traditional character – noted British architects' fear of flamboyance and personal expression. Eight years on, however, Hitchcock paid tribute to the completed cathedral, its assured sumptuousness and its uninhibited symbolism. It was those very factors, he pointed out, which simultaneously singled it out from the buildings designed by Spence's contemporaries and successfully captured the imagination of the wider public [**78**].[17]

Spence's career as designer of parish churches stemmed not from his work at Coventry Cathedral but from three small churches in suburban Coventry [**79**]. The first, and technically most adventurous, of his church commissions, these churches were designed in response to Bishop Gorton's concern to provide the new housing estates with a place of worship. For the churches at Tile Hill, Bell Green and Willenhall, Spence promised the Bishop a solution which was 'simple, direct, topical and traditional'.[18] The

77 Coventry Cathedral, Gethsemane Chapel, with panels by Steven Sykes and ironwork by Basil Spence
SC1029531 RCAHMS

78 Coventry Cathedral from the north with the Chapel of Industry (left) and the Chapel of Unity (right), *c*.1962
SC1029631 RCAHMS

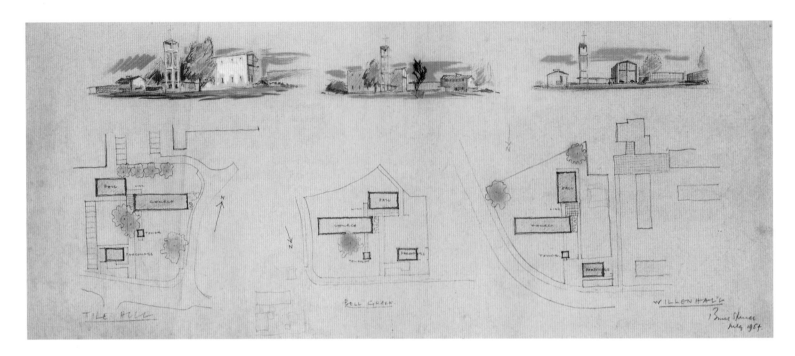

method of construction was unconventional, using the same technology – coarse mass concrete walling – which Wimpey's were using for the nearby housing. The design of all three was derived from the cathedral: a rectangular basilican-type church, fully glazed at one end, in which proportion and rhythm were established by a concrete portal frame. The impact of the design lay here and in the contrast between the rugged texture of the 'no-fines' concrete walling and the delicate church plate, robust timber furnishing and the abstract coloured pattern of the ceiling. In each church, the position of the altar was accentuated by the judicious use of natural light. These churches were linked by a covered way to a low-slung hall and an openwork concrete tower.

Their rapid and economical construction attracted commissions from the dioceses of Leicester, Sheffield and Manchester, where in the late 1950s Spence and his assistants designed similar groups of church, hall, tower and vicarage for suburban parishes. These churches – built of brick rather than concrete – were less harshly textured than those at Coventry. As at Coventry, however, everyday materials and simple finishes were enriched and dignified by judicious commissions for works of art and by careful attention to siting and planting. Both aspects were evident at St Aidan's Leicester, its façade dominated by a magnificent tile panel by William Gordon and its gaunt location softened

by the creation of a semi-enclosed garden and pool within an intimate cloister court. Elsewhere, notably at St Paul's, Ecclesfield, the influence of Scandinavian architecture came to the fore [80]. Glazed at each end, with cranked brick walls and a clerestory of plain glass above which the lightweight lattice-work roof appeared to float, the effect is of a church in which daylight and absence of pomp suggested a new idiom for the Anglican church. The success of this church lies in the character of its symbolism, conveyed in the progression from font to altar to the world visible beyond, and in the sobriety of its presentation of a place of worship in which nature serves as a trigger to prayer and contemplation.[19] These churches do not represent a re-thinking of the shape of the church in accordance with modern liturgical practice. Their achievement rather lies in the way in which they supplied the new suburban estates and their prairie planning with focal points, and countered the 'depressing expansiveness' of these places by their subtle provision of enclosure.[20]

In May 1956 Spence and his wife visited Le Corbusier's recently completed pilgrimage chapel of Notre-Dame du Haut, Ronchamp, in eastern France [81]. The lecture which Spence gave to the RIBA that autumn conveys the impact made on him by this extraordinary building.[21] Ronchamp triggered a new approach to spatial relationships, to materials, to light, and to the shape and layout of a

79 Design for three churches at Coventry: Tile Hill, Bell Green and Willenhall, 1954
DP011814 RCAHMS

It combines a concern to knit together chapel and setting by means of planting, water and landscape contours, with a new interest in the idea of a centralised worshipping space. Both were explored in Spence's last three religious buildings: the church of St Matthew, Reading, Mortonhall Crematorium, Edinburgh, and The Meeting House, University of Sussex.

St Matthew's, Spence's most innovative parish church in terms of layout, was conceived as an irregular polygon, made up of a series of overlapping masonry wall-slabs, which with two projecting concrete side-chapels and an integral bell-tower created a highly sculptural effect [**82**]. Realised in 1967 to a much simplified design made with the assistance of Spence's son John, the internal layout of the church suggests the impact of the liturgical movement, while the use of light dramatised the key elements of altar, font and pulpit within a crisp spatial envelope.[23]

At Mortonhall, Spence conceived a building in relation to the route of the visitor. The crematorium proper is tucked into the side of a hill, and the main approach skirts a tiny chapel of remembrance to reveal a small and a larger chapel in a woodland clearing, their southern walls rising in sharp profile like jagged masonry shards [**83, 85**]. The combination of angled walls and narrow window apertures and the use of indirect lighting was something which was explored by Spence across a range of building types during the 1960s. At Mortonhall – as at Reading – a pyramid on the roof of the large chapel functions as a vestigial spire, and admits light into the interior over the spot where the coffin rests during the funeral service [**84**]; a concrete cylinder performs the same role in the interior of the smaller chapel.[24]

The design of Mortonhall (1961–7) forms a bridge

80 St Paul's Church, Ecclesfield, 1959
Private collection

church. By this date, Coventry Cathedral was complete to the level of the nave floor, and Ronchamp's influence was registered only obliquely. However, during the next decade, in his unexecuted designs for university chapels and the crematorium chapel at Mortonhall, Spence could be more experimental. His proposal of 1958 for a chapel at the University of Edinburgh uses the rounded surfaces of apse and tower, inward-leaning walls and a butterfly roof to give a sense of space gently enfolded.[22] Three years later, Spence proposed an octagonal chapel comprising V-shaped buttress walls with full-height glazing for a courtyard at Durham University, sketching a free-standing cross nearby.

81 Notre-Dame du Haut, Ronchamp by Le Corbusier, 1955
Private collection

82 Model of St Matthew's Church, Reading, first scheme c.1963
SC1057400 RCAHMS

between Coventry Cathedral and the Sussex Meeting House (1963–7). Like Coventry, Mortonhall's angled walls rise above roof level [**85**]; its main chapel is illuminated by split buttresses filled with coloured glass, like those in the cathedral's Chapel of Unity. Although these buttresses, creating an effect of high drama, were not eventually used at the Meeting House, it is there that the motifs and ideas of the previous ten years come to fruition.[25] Within its circular plan – suggestive of chapter house and baptistery, oast house and dovecote, a theatre of debate and modern liturgy – the Meeting House accommodated both secular and religious functions, set slightly apart from the campus around it by a screen of trees and a reflecting moat [see **122, 125**].

These buildings reveal a different Spence from that of the cathedral, and a new preoccupation with the relationship between congregation and celebrant. Liverpool's Roman Catholic Cathedral, completed in 1967 to the design of Frederick Gibberd, registers the difference in liturgical thought since the Coventry competition, and the impact of the Second Vatican Council.[26] Liverpool, orientated around a central altar, is frequently used as a means of pointing up the shortcomings of Spence as church planner. Significantly, however, Spence (who helped to write the brief for Liverpool, and to assess the competition held in 1959) actually endorsed Gibberd's freedom to design for worship in the round. Gibberd followed Spence's example by commissioning leading contemporary artists and using stained glass to help unify and focus the gaunt interior which he created. Meanwhile, Spence – who had been denied the opportunity to experiment with a central worshipping space at Coventry – achieved at Mortonhall and Sussex in the same year more intimate but no less exciting buildings, with a surer handling of scale, light and interior space.

83 Elevation for Mortonhall Crematorium, 1961
DP021032 RCAHMS

84 Interior of Mortonhall Crematorium, 1967
SC778101 RCAHMS

opposite

85 Mortonhall Crematorium, Edinburgh, entrance
SC1031058 RCAHMS

BUILDING FOR MODERN CEREMONY

MILES GLENDINNING

In the architecture of the nineteenth and earlier centuries, the importance of any particular building type or individual project was shown by the degree of ornament or general stately grandeur: a clear, hierarchical system which could be understood by all.[1] In the new egalitarian post-war age, modern architecture generally tried its utmost to put those inequalities and hierarchies behind it. Its emblematic building types, such as mass housing or schools, were invested with as much architectural intensity of thought and status as any others. But, despite all these efforts and their accompanying rhetoric, there was still a strong residual feeling among many of the new civic or collective patrons that some building types needed to be set apart by something of the old hierarchical grandeur – whether to ennoble the new institutions of the welfare state, or to mask the decline of traditional institutions from Britain's imperial, capitalist past.[2]

For such a task, Spence's skills as an architect were ideally suited. Drawing both on his own training within the Beaux-Arts and the Arts and Crafts traditions, and also the more advanced programmatic modernist ethos of the talented young architects drawn to his own post-1951 practice, he was able to design institutional buildings of an often complex hybrid character, investing well-planned (social) administrative complexes with a touch of traditional character and charisma, either through the use of planning devices and architectural motifs, or even through more explicit use of 'ornament' or 'traditional style'. The wider architectural context for this approach was the discontent of many modern architects at the scientific 'aridity' of strict Functionalism: a disquiet that led to the 1940s and 1950s debates within CIAM (Congrès Internationaux d'Architecture Moderne) on 'monumentality' and 'humanity'.[3] During the early and mid-1950s Spence's design for Coventry Cathedral resoundingly established his credentials as a master of 'new monumentality', mingling as it did masonry and reinforced concrete construction; it also tellingly alluded to traditional motifs such as the Gothic 'fan vault' and made judicious use of flamboyant gestures such as the grand staircase or columned portico.

This chapter traces the way in which elements of traditional, stately monumentality, including the planning motifs of the courtyard, arcade and tower, were extended to secular, institutional buildings in a succession of projects from the late 1950s onwards – above all, in Spence's two most prestigious post-Coventry projects, the British Embassy in Rome (1959–71), and Hyde Park Cavalry Barracks [**86**], London (1959–70). During the 1950s, Spence began consistently to employ the courtyard as an ordering motif, with its connotations of tradition and stately grandeur. For example, his masterplan of 1955 for the University of Edinburgh combined an array of courtyards and towered punctuations, to give 'a vision … comparable with Cambridge' [see **117**]. His unbuilt project for Slough Municipal Buildings (1956–7) combined International Modern banded windows with a quadrangular courtyard plan form, and featured the theatrical gesture of a fountain-fronted blank stone wall occupying one whole side of the courtyard.[4] The same motif was expressed in a more overtly rugged form at Spence's Falmer House, Sussex University (completed 1962), with brick and concrete arches evoking ruined antiquity and integrating arcading and ornamental pools.

In parallel with this, Spence was also influenced by the movement within 1950s modern architecture advocating the enrichment of Functionalism by a restrained 'return to ornament'. Inspired especially by the late work of Frank Lloyd Wright, a range of architects in Italy, Britain, the USA and elsewhere sought to devise a more 'contextual' architecture inspired by Renaissance, Baroque or Gothic decoration.[5] The most triumphant realisation of a 'monumental Modernism' both of plan and decoration in the 1950s was the Lincoln Center for the Performing Arts in New York (designed from 1958, and built 1959–69): an ensemble of stately, somewhat classical institutions set around a formal piazza, arcaded or porticoed and faced in Roman travertine, in an attempt (as Philip Johnson put it in 1959) to look 'away from the International Style toward enriched forms'.[6]

In the context of Spence's own career, the British Embassy in Rome and the Hyde Park Barracks were the two

86 Hyde Park Cavalry Barracks, London, seen from the park
DP004585 RCAHMS

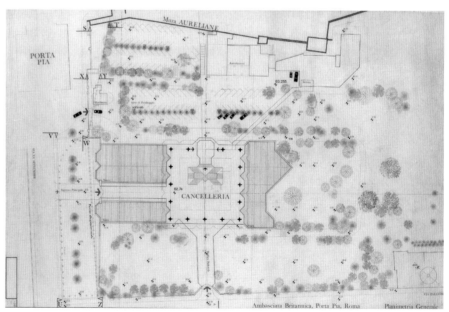

87 Design for the British Embassy, Rome showing its proximity to the Porta Pia, 1962
DP010913 RCAHMS

88 Site plan for the British Embassy, Rome, 1967
DP021648 RCAHMS

major projects of grand, national symbolism which followed his work on Coventry Cathedral. He reorganised his practice in 1963 to be able to devote maximum attention to them. The two projects ran almost in parallel, starting in earnest in 1959 and taking up the whole of the 1960s. Both were commissioned by the government for prestigious and socially conservative user groups – cavalry guardsmen and diplomats – on elite sites that would inevitably excite opposition from amenity interests, and both suffered the difficulties in gaining approval and in construction that were common to many high-prestige public-sector projects. But there were equally important differences. Both set out to deploy 'traditional' motifs, but in radically different ways: while the embassy in Rome was an isolated pavilion evoking the layout and detail of a Roman Renaissance palazzo in a garden, Hyde Park was really a chunk of city, embedded in the wider urban fabric, and whose design integrated 'ornamental' elements within a highly complex, multi-level building group. And this urban context was not just any part of any city, but the wealthiest part of London; and the barracks' occupants, however much an army elite, were also viewed by some neighbours in anti-social terms. In October 1960, for example, the residents of the exclusive adjoining Albert Gate Mansions lobbied against any increase in the smell from the horses stabled on site.

Today, embassy buildings have two main roles – administration and symbolic representation; the nineteenth-century concept of the ambassador as an active, semi-autonomous agent is defunct. Under the mid-twentieth-century modern movement, with its great diversity of architectural philosophies and its strong utopian overtones, the design of 'chancery' buildings (the main public part of an embassy) became the vehicle to convey, consciously or unconsciously, a variety of messages about national identity, the mutual relationship of states, and other political or cultural themes. These included the tension between the assertion of one's own country and respect for the host country, and achieving the architectural balance between 'closed' and 'open' character. Most embassies were, however, still housed in existing buildings, not least in historical areas such as Rome. The new Rome chancery was essentially an office building, located for security reasons on a closed, fenced-in site. But its location, in gardens immediately beside Michelangelo's Porta Pia and the Roman Aurelian Wall, was one of unparalleled cultural prestige and sensitivity [87, 88].

The previous chancery building on the site had been blown up in 1946 by Jewish 'Irgun' terrorists, after which the cleared site was zoned as a park by the Rome authorities, requiring extreme tact to secure the change in the city's development plan (*piano regolatore*) that would allow a replacement building. But the overwhelming concern to 'do it right' in Rome stemmed both from the political alliance of Britain and Italy and the more general northern European respect for Italian and Roman culture. In 1971 Evelyn Shuckburgh, ambassador during the decisive pre-construction and early construction phase at Rome, contrasted the general decline in the number and size of embassies, owing to 'our lesser weight in world affairs', with the need for special treatment at Rome, a grade-one embassy in a key location; the chancery project would have to convey the full prestige of an embassy. He stressed that as 'Italians attach importance to appearances', buildings in grand styles would be 'not wasted in Italy'.[7] This historic, sensitive location, confronted the project with very strongly organised potential opposition. The site had first been proposed for rebuilding in 1950, in the utilitarian modernist style of the in-house government Ministry of Works architects. But the scheme, despite being

resubmitted several times, had been repeatedly turned down by the many-layered Italian heritage and planning bodies. Acknowledging the exceptional site, in 1957 the Ministry of Works had hit on the idea of appointing Spence, as an architect uniquely skilled in 'modern monumentality' and effective juxtaposition of the new and old.

Spence was officially appointed by the Foreign Office in 1959, and set to work personally on the design in 1960–1, envisaging it as his chief architectural challenge following the imminent completion of Coventry Cathedral. To further underline the seriousness of the British attitude to the project, Pier Luigi Nervi was appointed Italian consultant, in this case with no active design role, but purely as a prestigious liaison figure with invaluable local knowledge. Spence rapidly arrived at a general design concept in response to the sensitive site. He cast the building as a low, compact two-storey block, massive and self-contained and detailed in a variegated, late-modernist manner, but raised up a full storey on slender single columns to allow the garden space to flow beneath it (a constructional device he also adopted in 1958–9 for his twenty-storey slab blocks in Glasgow's Gorbals). Although possibly influenced by the designs of some recent US embassies, especially the courtyard plan and open ground floor of Harry Weese's Accra, Ghana (1956–9), the imagery and metaphors here were in some ways more overtly 'traditional'. The plan comprised a square of sixteen sections joined 'like a necklace', each supported by a single column. Of the two floors above, the first floor had the larger, grander rooms, and the top floor the smaller offices; the highly symmetrical plan prevented any direct expression of the normal threefold split in a chancery's functions: public areas, chancery division offices and secure zone. Construction comprised a reinforced concrete frame with set-forward travertine cladding of a 'Baroque' character very similar to some 1950s set pieces such as the Lincoln Center, New York.[8]

Spence's descriptions emphasised, with characteristic passion, the historically rooted character of this 'modern palazzo in travertine'. It would be 'an object of quality set in a garden with ample space around and through it, a light but strongly modelled structure that is modern and yet stems from the same trunk as Michelangelo's Porta Pia'; it would, indeed, 'with one hand stretch back to Roman times and, with the other, grasp the present day. The building must have classical unity, beautiful materials, expert craftsmanship; it must have the Roman scale and the same "blood group" as its immediate surroundings'.[9] He himself argued in a letter, dated 1961, to ambassador Sir Ashley Clarke that 'the main objective is to create a symbol representative of Great Britain in a foreign capital, but with a difference, as Rome may be considered to be the cradle of our modern civilisation. A secondary objective is to provide an embassy office building which is efficient. It must look "right". It should, if possible, excite admiration from the Italians and should not dismay our own people. It should harmonise with the unique surroundings, in scale, rhythm and materials.' In an article in the *Daily Express*, Spence put the challenge more bluntly: as the embassy was 'our own little piece of Britain in Rome', it was essential to show sensitivity towards the existing landscape, to ensure that the British were not 'shown up as a lot of cultural barbarians'.[10]

But Spence was not content merely with a modestly contextual approach. With the Porta Pia next door, he saw some flamboyant gesture as essential – yet any 'grand' elements would at the same time have to be tasteful and discreet. In a master-stroke of ingenuity, his enclosed palazzo concept made it possible to include one rhetorically stately element, a sweeping, somewhat Baroque external entrance staircase – entirely hidden from public view, within the central courtyard [**91**]. Weese had included a similar feature on a much smaller site at Accra, and Spence's Slough plan echoed the same idea indirectly in its blank 'fountain wall'. Spence's concept of a modern palazzo 'floating' in the landscape [**92**] proved perfectly attuned to the expectations of the Italian officialdom, and his presentation of a model of the scheme to a forty-five-strong consultative municipal vetting panel of planners, architects and officials, at an hour-and-a-half long meeting in September of 1962 was met with a standing ovation: final approval from the Consiglio Comunale came eventually on 28 May 1963.[11]

Having triumphantly overcome Italian official opposition, Spence was faced with far more serious governmental pressures in Britain, especially during the financial crisis that engulfed the post-1964 Wilson Labour Government. As a result, construction of the embassy was delayed until 1968–71; a disorientating time lag which disguised the fact that the design was, essentially, a sensitive yet stately set piece of late 1950s 'contextual', 'ornamental' modernism, fine-tuned to the status of Rome as a universal seat of culture. Spence's design should most properly be compared not to the great

public buildings of the 1960s and early 1970s, such as Denys Lasdun's National Theatre of 1965–76, but to the Lincoln Center, which was also conceived in the late 1950s.[12]

For much the same reasons of government cutbacks within the uncertain post-war setting of Britain, Spence's Hyde Park Cavalry Barracks project followed a similar protracted trajectory, with an inception and development phase in 1957–62 followed by lengthy cost uncertainty in the mid-1960s and eventual construction in 1967–70. However, its response to the challenge of 'ceremonial' design was dominated by a different strand of 1950s modernism from the stateliness of Rome: namely, the move within British urban planning and redevelopment towards a more complex, densely mixed urbanity, incorporating forms such as multi-layered mega structures, street decks and cluster or spine planning. Within public housing, tower blocks remained a prominent feature, but were now integrated into denser complexes, such as Chamberlin, Powell & Bon's Barbican

89 Construction of the gateway to the British Embassy, Rome, in progress, 1971
SC1057799 RCAHMS

90 Exterior of the newly-completed British Embassy, Rome, showing the fountain and pool
SC1057783 RCAHMS

91 Interior of the British Embassy courtyard, Rome
SC1057776 RCAHMS

92 Aerial view of the British Embassy and the grounds showing the entrance from the Via XX Settembre
SC1057802 RCAHMS

93 The late Victorian barracks complex that preceded Spence's Hyde Park Cavalry Barracks, London
DP027042 RCAHMS

(built from 1962). There was sometimes also an attempt to reflect the muddle of the previously reviled Victorian city, not least through traditional materials such as red-brick.[13]

The 'client' for this complex project was one of the most prestigious groups within the British establishment: The Household Cavalry, which consists of The Life Guards and The Blues and Royals (Royal Horse Guard and 1st The Royal Dragoons), is the ceremonial elite of the British Army. Having been housed for several decades in the dilapidated setting

94 Composite elevation of Hyde Park Cavalry Barracks, London, c.1965
DP027043 RCAHMS

of the late nineteenth-century Hyde Park Barracks [**93**], in 1957 the regiments' commander approached Spence about the possible redevelopment of the barracks on this unusual – very slender – site set in a location of extreme landscape sensitivity on the south side of Hyde Park. Spence was probably recommended by Lord Mountbatten, who knew him well from numerous official functions. He was also on good terms with the new War Office chief architect, Donald Gibson (Coventry's City Architect until 1955), who wrote informally to him in 1959, making clear the exceptional 'artistic' status accorded to this project, and stressing that Spence should design in a way that added 'beauty' and 'art' to the basic barracks carcase: 'It is my hope that (within the cost limits) you will feel free … to invest some of your money in the more enjoyable things of life.'[14]

The challenge faced by Spence and his design team, including Anthony Blee as chief assistant, was to accommodate on this pencil-thin site a formidable range of horse-related functions, including stables, stable yard (or parade ground; to accommodate two regiments in full parade order), riding school and forage barn, together with a complex programme for the 'human' accommodation, including three messes and linked accommodation: the need was essentially for a high-density housing project, with other functions and elements of exaggerated stateliness all embedded within it. It quickly became clear that all the requirements except one could be easily satisfied by a low or medium-height structure in decked form, set above a podium base exploiting the north–south fall of the ground to create a lower ground-floor vehicular service level facing Knightsbridge. The one exception was the need to accommodate a large number of other ranks' married quarters. It was agreed by all that the minimum requirement for the daily functioning of the on-site element of the regiment was 120 flats, but shortage of army flats for married couples in

H	G	F	E	D	C	B	A
OFFICERS' MESS	MARRIED OFFICERS' MAISONETTES CAR PARKING STORAGE FOR FLATS	SQUASH COURTS MARRIED ORs' FLATS LAUNDRETTE	PLAYGROUND RIDING SCHOOL	W.O.'S MESS & CHANGING ROOM GYMNASIUM BAND PRACTICE ROOM RIFLE RANGE	BARRACKS OFFICERS' OFFICES GUARD ROOM MEDICAL UNIT	NAAFI—ORs' MESS FORGE & CHANGING ROOM REGIMENTAL STORES & FORAGE BARN LOADING BAY	STABLES FORAGE

95 Early design model for
Hyde Park Cavalry Barracks,
London, 1964
SC1056983 RCAHMS

central London made it highly desirable to include more, and
the initial commissioning letter suggested 170.[15]

The simplest solution to the married quarters problem at
Hyde Park was to group all the flats together into a single tall
block, and Spence immediately began to explore this pos-
sibility. A sketch of April 1960 indicates in outline the layout
which was eventually used, with the stables at the east end,
and the residential and communal accommodation strung
out to the west, with a tall tower rising from the centre [**94**].
By going for a tower, Spence immediately projected the
scheme into a lively debate about tall buildings in central

London, especially those overlooking the royal parks. At
Hyde Park, the tower solution was driven forward by the
demands for 'a terrific number of married quarters – there
was never any getting away from that!' and by Spence's own
personal preference for a vertical accent in this otherwise
concentrated horizontal complex.

Between 1960 and 1962, chiefly in response to anxiety
within the government planning watchdog, the Royal Fine
Art Commission (RFAC), over the sensitive location – just as
in Rome – Spence offered a succession of alternative proposals for the tower, mostly at first in perspective form.

96 Hyde Park Cavalry
Barracks' canteen
SC1057011 RCAHMS

97 Hyde Park Cavalry
Barracks, London
DP005487 RCAHMS

A horizontal version of the married quarters in the form of an 'elephantine' slab block was also sketched out, and rapidly ruled out, to Spence and Blee's relief. The various tower permutations allowed for between 120 and 175 flats. In early July 1962, after Spence had produced further alternative perspectives, the debates on the form and cost of the tower culminated in a final radical change of plan. Instructed definitively by the War Office to plan once again for the basic minimum number of 120 married flats, Blee and the project architect, John Church, finally devised a plan for a 'simple, square, slimmer, taller tower'. The new tower would still be ninety-seven metres high, but would have only four flats on each floor above podium level 97]. And at the top there would be several floors of officers' flats, crowned by the officers' mess – a bizarre location for the latter, given the ceremonial requirement for a heavy 'drum horse' to be ridden up to the mess entrance (which would require a special, strengthened lift). Spence immediately adjusted his advocacy language to fit the new scheme, comparing the townscape effect of the slender 'pencil' block to the towers of the Palace of Westminster or the Pagoda at Kew Gardens.[16]

In his final design, Spence carefully integrated the disparate elements of the complex into an architecturally coherent whole. Once the key ceremonial planning requirement of the parade ground had been established, the decked accommodation could then be distributed along the site from east to west, so as to slide functionally from stables to family accommodation, and in rank from other ranks to officers: common sense soon prevailed over the officers' mess, which was shifted down to the main podium. The enclosed character of the nineteenth-century barracks was replaced by a more outward looking and (apart from the tower) smaller-scale approach. Each of the new elements – the stables (planned innovatively on two floors), the various messes, the barracks block, the married quarters' tower, the riding school and the officers' flats – was expressed in a distinct manner, in the traditional 'mixed development' manner of British public housing. Internally, too, there was differentiation, from the four-man rooms of the barracks block to the unified interior of the officers' mess. But unlike the mound-like massing of much dense early 1960s housing, the ninety-four metre high tower was set apart in a more traditional manner, like a church tower, with an aerodynamically profiled top, so as 'to read as a true tower, with a proper base, a definite body and a head which would cut a good silhouette against the sky'.[17] At Coventry, there was no need to add another tower;

here, he could more than make up for that, on one of Central London's most prominent sites. Typically of Spence's liking for gestures of 'architecture parlante', the crest of the tower distinctly resembled a guardsman's helmet.

The vertical layering of the site helped weld together these diverse functions in a differentiated yet monumental way, with due allowance for the ceremonial set pieces. The public and service character of the ground floor and lower ground floor levels – where horses and vehicles would predominate – was expressed by a generally open concrete column and beam finish, with the first level spanned by thick cross beams and precast arched shell ceilings (which had originally been designed for the University of Sussex) whose height would allow a mounted soldier in ceremonial uniform to pass beneath. The officers' mess was treated as a fluid yet stately space, spanned dramatically by a concrete minstrel's gallery. Above the platform level, the more private and segregated nature of the different functional and rank areas was expressed through the greater solidity of brick masonry walls punctuated by relatively small openings – although the tower block was set apart by its banded windows and precast cladding.[18]

After a protracted process of approval, building work at Hyde Park Barracks eventually started in 1967, but the highly individualistic character of the project, and the prestige of the 'clients', made cost overruns almost inevitable, just

as at Rome. Project architect John Church recalled that: 'When you had someone of the stature of Lord Mountbatten directly involving himself, and asking for specific changes and costly enhancements, you weren't going to say to him, "Hold on, I need to check with the Ministry!" You'd just issue the variation order!' When the Queen visited the barracks in 1971 after completion, she 'greeted Basil … and before the Commanding Officer could do his formal introduction, she said, looking over Basil's shoulder at the tower, "Well, Sir Basil, whatever are you going to do next?" – with a note of slight foreboding in her voice! Without a second's hesitation, he replied, "Duck and run for cover, Ma'am!" – and she doubled up with laughter!'[19] But, by 1970, all kinds of large modernist complexes, even those designed with careful acknowledgement of 'traditional' elements, had fallen completely from public favour: only after another decade or so, in the postmodern eclecticism of the 1970s and 1980s, would a skill in reconciling modernity and tradition, and offsetting the everyday with touches of the theatrical, become truly central to architecture.

98 Kit layout diagram for officers' quarters, Hyde Park Cavalry Barracks, London, c.1966
DP009478 RCAHMS

99 Section through the Riding School, Hyde Park Cavalry Barracks, London, 1965
DP009492 RCAHMS

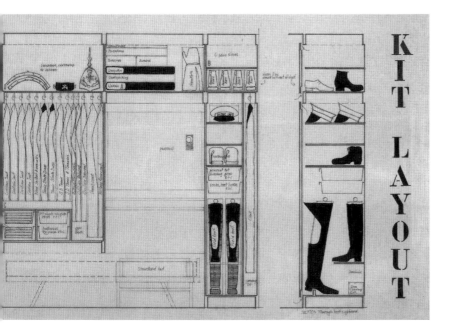

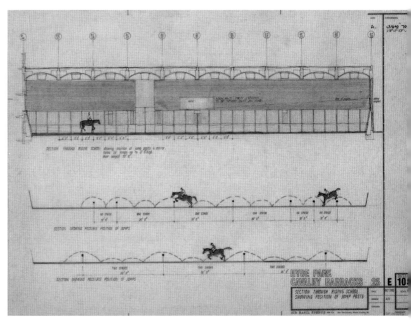

FROM GENIUS LOCI TO THE GORBALS
SPENCE AS ARCHITECT OF MASS HOUSING

MILES GLENDINNING

The overwhelming centre of gravity of post-war reconstruction in the UK, as elsewhere in Europe, was the 'national programme' of mass housing. Britain, especially Scotland, was unusual in Europe in that most of this mass housing was directly built and owned by local municipal authorities – something which, with the strong traditions of civic pride and autonomy in Britain, allowed for a surprising variety of organisational approaches and architectural solutions.

In locational and planning terms, the 'national housing drive' polarised into two complementary elements: the building of new, relatively low-density settlements on 'greenfield' sites in the suburbs of existing towns or in completely new towns; and the redevelopment and intensification of existing inner-urban sites, clearing away obsolete 'slum' areas. On the whole, the housing projects built on both these two types of site were designed by specialist housing architects, employed either directly by public authorities or by house-building firms, or by private practices specialising in housing and social architecture. In their work, often pedestrian in character but sometimes more intellectually elevated, consistent lines of development in house-types or layouts could be followed over many years.[1]

Basil Spence, by contrast, took on commissions for housing – some small, some very prominent – on an ad hoc basis, and thus each one was designed largely from first principles – somewhat like his great public buildings, and in striking contrast to the consistency of his English civic universities or parish churches. All the same, the broad trends of post-war mass housing were perceptible in his projects, including a shift from relatively low-density, spacious building for 'general needs' in the 1940s to an increasing focus on redevelopment of more 'difficult' urban sites – some in historic towns – from the 1950s. At the same time as this rather incremental process, however, another more dramatic polarisation can be identified within Spence's housing work: between one overwhelmingly forceful and monumental project, for redevelopment of part of Glasgow's Gorbals slum area [100] using massive, twenty-storey slab blocks (1958–65), and all the other projects, which adopted,

by comparison, a moderate, conciliatory, low-rise approach, whether in the design of new greenfield developments or contextual inner-urban interventions.

Spence's first post-Second World War housing commissions were secured in the mid –1940s, during the period of transition towards the establishment of his own separate private practice. He began by building, at almost opposite ends of Britain, four quite substantial projects – two at Sunbury (Middlesex); one at Selkirk, south of Edinburgh; and one at Dunbar, a fishing port east of the Scottish capital on the East Lothian coast – that represented very well the most advanced trends of modernist greenfield housing design. These were structured by the somewhat utopian concern to foster 'community' through planning in self-contained 'neighbourhoods', separated from each other by careful green landscaping in the English picturesque tradition, and planned in hierarchical arrangements of housing groups and local services, so as to maximise sunlight and open air. This planning approach, strongly hinted at in C. van Eesteren's garden-city general development plan for Amsterdam (approved in 1939), had been elaborated in some detail towards the end of the war in Britain by William Holford's research team within the Ministry of Town and Country Planning, with a view to application 'on the ground' in the New Towns envisaged in Patrick Abercrombie's Greater London Plan (1944). Especially influential had been Peter Shepheard's hypothetical plan of 1945 for a New Town at Ongar, envisaging six neighbourhoods of 10,000 inhabitants, each comprising a hierarchy of landscaped spaces and housing groups, arranged in parallel rows (or *Zeilenbau*) at right angles to roads, to maximise sunlight penetration, and help separate pedestrians and vehicles; the diversity of households would be reflected in contrasting building types, with flats intended for smaller households and low-rise terrace houses for families.[2]

Of the early post-war schemes, the two built for Sunbury Urban District Council (Laleham Road, 1948–9, 164 dwellings; and Beechwood Avenue, 1950–2, 190 dwellings) were slightly more conservative in layout.[3] Both featured a loop

100 A view from ground level of the hanging balconies of Hutchesontown 'C', the Gorbals, Glasgow, 1965
SC438977 RCAHMS

road, ringed by permutations of single-storey old people's houses, two-storey cottages and three-storey flats, built of brick colour-washed in various shades, and with aluminium roofs, trellises and door canopies [**101**]. At Laleham Road, the loop road was lined with staggered semi-detached pairs of cottages, with more varied house-types arranged around square-like spaces at the centre and east; at Beechwood Avenue, the centre of the development comprised a group of terraces arranged more boldly in *Zeilenbau* rows, with allotments adjacent. Internally, the four- and five-apartment family houses in the terraces tried to move towards a more flowing spatial arrangement: the open-plan ground floor had a dining recess in the living room. Selkirk Town Council's Bannerfield scheme (awarded in 1945 to Spence when still part of Rowand Anderson & Paul & Partners) was an altogether more ambitious concern, containing 300 dwellings in a multi-phase development, with construction of a 120-dwelling first phase beginning in 1947, and the whole development finished in 1963 [**102**]. By comparison with the flat Middlesex sites, Bannerfield benefited from a more dramatic hilly, wooded setting. The larger scale of the development allowed a more consistent modernist planning, with two-storey terraced houses arranged in *Zeilenbau* style on each side of the main east–west road, culs-de-sac in the north-west part of the scheme, and two three-storey blocks containing small flats. Bannerfield contrasted with Sunbury also in the more substantial-looking materials, with roughcast brick and precast concrete details; some houses featured somewhat 'Mackintosh-style' projecting chimney stacks rising from ground level. Roofs in the first phase were aluminium, but tiles and slates were used later; as development of the scheme progressed, the less lavish subsidy regime of the mid- and late 1950s made necessary a simplification of the detailing. The Summerfield development in Dunbar was very similar to Bannerfield in its layout and architectural appearance as well as its size and date (also 300 dwellings and 1945).[4]

Essentially, these four projects formed part of the mainstream of 'architecturally progressive' 1940s low-rise housing design – a kind of early mixed development without sharp contrasts of dwelling types, as exemplified most famously in Frederick Gibberd's Shacklewell Road / Somerford Grove development in Hackney (1946–7), the London County Council's (LCC's) Lansbury demonstration housing project of 1948–51 in east London (designed by various private architects), or the early sections of Mk. I New Towns such as Harlow, Stevenage

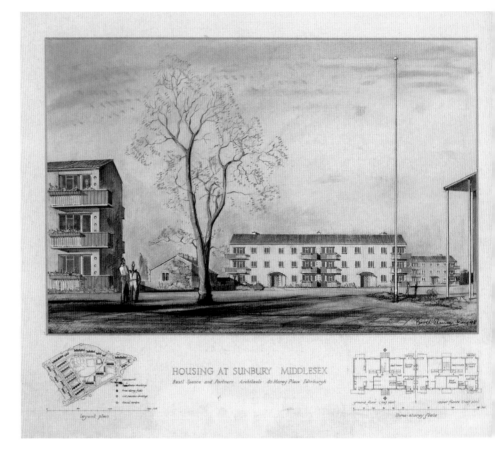

HOUSING AT SUNBURY MIDDLESEX

Basil Spence and Partners Architects 46 Moray Place Edinburgh

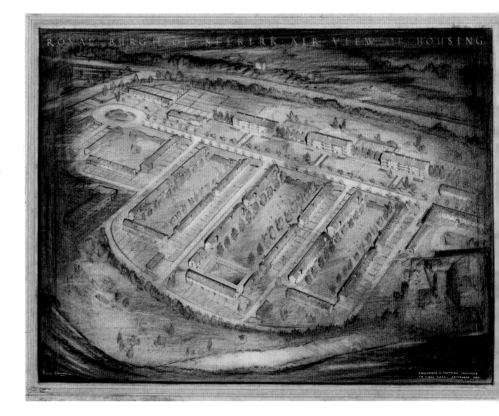

101 Design for housing scheme at Sunbury, Middlesex, 1948
DP012265 RCAHMS

102 Design for Bannerfield housing estate, Selkirk, 1946
DP012301 RCAHMS

103 Victoria Street, Dunbar
SC684939 RCAHMS

104 Crookfur Cottage Homes
SC1058151 RCAHMS

or East Kilbride.[5] However, when Spence actually came to design a sub-neighbourhood in a New Town in the late 1950s – Area 7 of the Vange neighbourhood at Basildon New Town – his approach had moved on, to reflect the growing insistence on pedestrian–vehicle segregation, including the 'Radburn' system of separate access footpaths. Originally, the Vange 7 project had also reflected architects' growing fascination with more radical contrasts of building types, by including a high tower block of small flats juxtaposed with low-rise terraces, but the government financial restraints of the late 1950s necessitated the substitution of cheaper three-storey blocks to house the small flats. As a result, eventually the building types at Vange 7 – a mixture of two-storey terraces, one-storey old people's houses and low-rise flats – was very much the same as that of the late 1940s.[6] By contrast, Spence's design for a group of charitable retirement homes for the drapery trade on the outskirts of Glasgow, Crookfur Cottage Homes (1964–7), openly acknowledged the 1960 taste for more irregular and close-packed low-rise housing, in harled styles with vernacular overtones [**104**]. The original concept was for an old people's 'village' in a wooded setting: a two-storey block of central services was surrounded by low terraces of cottages in irregular, staggered groupings. The *Architectural Review* argued that the houses 'come near to whimsy in their calculated charm, which is straight out of almshouse vernacular, but the inhabitants are delighted'.[7]

In parallel with this succession of respectably up-to-date projects for greenfield sites, Spence was also making a far more innovative contribution to housing design in the contrasting area of piecemeal redevelopment in historic towns. This was a field which enjoyed roots stretching back well over half a century in the Edinburgh Old Town, where Patrick Geddes and his successors (notably his son-in-law, Frank Mears, Spence's planning tutor at Edinburgh College of Art) had incessantly proselytised a philosophy of restrained modern intervention in the historic fabric – 'conservative surgery' – influenced both by the sanitary drive to open up green spaces in congested 'slums', and by the Arts and Crafts philosophy of place-sensitive and material-sensitive picturesque. It was Spence's personal achievement to have successfully evolved, in the 1940s, a new formula of historic-burgh redevelopment integrated fully with contemporary trends in the modern movement, especially that strand of international modernism since the 1930s which emphasised use of 'vernacular' or 'humanist' materials.[8]

This achievement was epitomised above all in Spence's post-war regeneration work in the centre of Dunbar, in parallel with the development of the greenfield site at Summerfield. Dunbar's town council had been busily redeveloping its decayed historic core from the 1930s. Here, the simplified Arts and Crafts cottage vernacular of the firm's pre-war terrace development (1934–6, designed by Kininmonth) contrasted strongly with the informal

modernism of post-war Victoria Street (1949–52, with an extension in 1955–6). The latter was intended for fisher families: four pocket-sized sites were filled by a complex mixture of linked two- and three-storey blocks containing twenty flats and maisonettes [103]. Their brick walling was partly rendered and partly clad in a local red sandstone rubble with bold external concrete stairs and local red-clay pantiled roof.[9]

This Dunbar scheme, following extensive and skilful publicity, including a striking perspective at the 1951 Royal Scottish Academy, and a Saltire Award for the same year, served as a springboard to a succession of 'conservative surgery' projects in Edinburgh itself. These began in 1952 with a commission for Edinburgh Corporation to prepare a conservation-conscious master plan for the regeneration of the dilapidated Forth-side villages of Cramond and Newhaven – projects in the broad European tradition of Old Town regeneration (*Altstadt-Sanierung*), including a mixture of preservation, clearance of rear accretions, and new infill 'in character'.[10] At Newhaven, this planning evaluation work was followed by selective preservation of some traditional fishermen's houses, with their forestairs, and a succession of infill redevelopments on the same general pattern as

Dunbar, including a complex of stepped, two- and three-storey houses and flats, with some stone walling, on a sloping site at Great Michael Rise (built 1957–9). These included a reinforced concrete framed five-storey-and-basement block of flats and (at right angles) a two-storey terrace; cladding in recycled stone setts gave the required 'local' or 'Scottish' character [105].[11]

By the start of the 1960s, these programmes of consistent 'vernacular' redevelopment housing had begun to seem old-fashioned and simplistic, in the face of the 'endless … possibilities' of grouping of high-density urban housing.[12] Accordingly, Spence's two major 1960s projects for Edinburgh Corporation, at East Claremont Street (sixty-three dwellings, built 1960–2) and Canongate / Lochend's Close / Reid's Court (thirty dwellings, 1961–9, on two adjacent sites on the north side of Canongate) were far more strongly polarised in approach. Perhaps to reflect its genius loci, East Claremont Street, located on the (then) dingy north-west edge of the New Town, was laid out largely in low, rectilinear groupings of L-planned three- and four-storey blocks around courtyards, built largely of colour-washed brick with orthodox international modern horizontal banded windows [106]. Canongate, in strong contrast, set out to address its

105 Newhaven housing, Edinburgh
Private collection

106 East Claremont Street, Edinburgh
SC1073012 RCAHMS

opposite

107 Presentation drawing showing Canongate housing project, Edinburgh *c.*1965
SC792276 RCAHMS

108 Housing at Brown's Close, Canongate, showing staircase detail
SC1031101 RCAHMS

109 Canongate housing project newly completed. Seen from south-east in its streetscape context
SC684956 RCAHMS

ROYAL MILE REDEVELOPMENT
79 - 121 Canongate

Old Town context directly – and in a far more assertive way than the genteel 'Empiricist' infills of the 1950s and early 1960s by Robert Hurd and others. Spence's design, arrived at after numerous personal reworkings, carefully threaded a line between contextual and confrontational approaches. On the one hand, Spence intended the Canongate project to be 'a slabby pierced wall thing, which ought to be in harmony with the old work': there were ground floor arcades, small, irregular upper-floor windows and harled / rubble facings.[13] At

the same time, there were calculatedly contrasting features, such as modernist monopitch roofs and a bold concrete rear staircase [**107**, **108**, **109**].

All these Edinburgh and 'East Coast' redevelopments, despite their variety of detailed planning and style, formed part of the general Geddesian tradition of modestly scaled contextual infill, but when in early 1958 Spence, along with his former classmate from Edinburgh College of Art, Robert Matthew, was presented with the opportunity to design the

centrepieces of Glasgow Corporation's redevelopment of the notorious Gorbals district, he chose to strike out in a very different direction, addressing 'context' only through general poetic metaphors of slum community – a new trend, pioneered earlier in the 1950s by architects such as the Smithsons or James Stirling.

At the Gorbals, Spence and Matthew were confronted with a soggy riverside site that would require extensive piling for any building higher than four storeys – a situation which greatly encouraged polarisation of new dwellings into either low-rise flats or very high, very concentrated blocks. Matthew's layout, in typical London County Council 'mixed development' style, accommodated a variety of dwelling types in a mixture of four-storey terraces and eighteen-storey tower blocks. Spence, however, boldly chose to concentrate his entire project into two enormous twenty-storey slab blocks, one long and one short (the Corporation having proposed three more conventional slabs). In flamboyant opposition to the general dominance of post-war Glasgow council housing by repetitive blocks designed by engineers or 'package deal' builders, Spence designed these blocks in an extravagantly articulated form, inspired in its general ruggedness by Le Corbusier's Unité d'Habitation, Marseille (1952), and also more specifically by Kunio Maekawa's monumental Harumi slab housing of 1958 in Tokyo.[14] He was initially assisted by Michael Blee and Derek Cobb in his Canonbury office, with Charles Robertson following up with the detailed execution of the design in Canonbury and Edinburgh, and overseeing the building process in Glasgow.

Although he had, by this stage, designed a number of high blocks for other purposes, Spence's only previous essay in multi-storey housing design had been an unexecuted project of 1950, nearly a decade earlier, for slab blocks containing workers' hostels, in the somewhat unlikely

110 Hutchesontown 'C', Gorbals, Glasgow, 1965
SC1052251 RCAHMS

111 Proposal for Spence's Newton Aycliffe multi-storey project, 1950
Private collection

112 Aerial view of Hutchesontown, Gorbals redevelopment in progress: Spence's Area 'C' and Robert Matthew's Area 'B' (with four towers) are seen near completion at the centre. The towers of the Scottish Special Housing Association Area 'D' are in the left foreground.
SC1052232 RCAHMS

low-density setting of the New Town of Newton Aycliffe, near Darlington [111].[15] These unbuilt blocks were only half the height of the Gorbals blocks, but they showed that the idea of great slabs in open space was already well lodged in Spence's mind.

Each of Spence's two Gorbals slabs was made up of a row of twenty-storey towers in reinforced concrete construction, each forty foot square, and linked by communal balconies or 'garden slabs' [113]. Each tower contained forty maisonettes (flats on two floors), on the Unité model: all bedrooms faced north and all living-rooms south, and each garden slab served four flats (accessed through the kitchens). With an eye to the traditional sensibilities of the Glasgow councillors on the Housing Committee, Spence argued colourfully that these 'hanging gardens' would reproduce the supposed communal spirit of the nineteenth-century Glasgow tenements in the new high-rise context: he told the Housing Committee that 'on Tuesdays, when all the washing's out,

it'll be like a great ship in full sail!' As five different sizes of flats were included in the brief, the internal planning of the interlocking maisonettes was of great complexity. Constructionally, this complexity was accommodated in a structural system of in-situ reinforced concrete box-frames, with specially designed cladding slabs.[16]

The engineering demands of all this were naturally quite challenging, and even the skilled Ove Arup's staff proved unable to find a structural solution for Spence's initial concept that the towers should be supported on a line of single columns, rather like his British Embassy in Rome (being designed at roughly the same time); eventually, pairs of slanting columns were substituted instead [114]. All this complex individualism inevitably cost significantly more than normal council housing – over £3,000 per dwelling, as opposed to the normal Scottish Office-approved ceiling of £2,800. Although Glasgow Corporation's powerful Housing Committee, led from 1959 by the city's messianic 'housing

113 Design for the shopping centre to the south of Hutchesontown 'C', Gorbals, Glasgow, 1958, which was eventually built to the design of Ian Burke, Martin & Partners
SC756210 RCAHMS

crusader', David Gibson, was normally concerned only with output, speed and economy in its council-housing construction programme, on this uniquely prestigious site an exception was made, and city architect Archibald Jury forcefully pressurised the Scottish Office to sanction Spence's complex design, arguing successfully that a royal foundation-laying had already been booked, and that an immediate start of work was imperative![17]

Eventually, in 1961, the foundation-laying ceremony duly took place, with Jury and Gibson in attendance along with Lord Provost Jean Roberts. Spence was also given a commission for a light industry area immediately to the north; a multi-level decked shopping centre immediately to the south was eventually designed in simplified form by Ian Burke, Martin & Partners.[18] For the first ten or so years Hutchesontown 'C' functioned more or less as intended, and enjoyed a reasonable popularity with its occupants. But, even before its completion, the architectural fashion had swung violently against any kind of high blocks and, as early as 1967, it was singled out for attack in the *Architectural Review* by critic Nicholas Taylor as a prime example of 'The Failure of "Housing"'.[19] The project's extreme complexity

made it very difficult to maintain properly, and it soon fell into disrepair; eventually, after half-hearted attempts at improvement or rehabilitation, the blocks were blown up in 1993, in a botched operation in which a local resident was killed by flying rubble.[20]

Hutchesontown 'C' is the only one of Spence's housing developments to have been demolished. Equally, it was the only one which did not conform to his accustomed pattern of contextual, modestly scaled modernity. Hutchesontown 'C', with its extravagantly sculptural form and the flamboyantly poetic metaphors used by Spence to advocate it, was in many ways a harbinger of the gestural, exaggerated individualism of much contemporary architecture of the last few years, since the revival of modernism in the late 1990s. Within Spence's own oeuvre, its forceful metaphoric character put it alongside projects such as the Expo '67 pavilion rather than more conventionally monumental projects, such as Coventry or Rome, where he was held back by a degree of respect for stately tradition. Perhaps, then, the short life and unhappy fate of Hutchesontown 'C' can serve as an appropriate warning to would-be 'iconic' projects of the present day, such as Enric Miralles's new Scottish Parliament.

114 Hutchesontown 'C', Gorbals, Glasgow, newly completed in 1966
SC1052311 RCAHMS

115 Hutchesontown 'C' featured on the cover of *Bauwelt* magazine, September 1966
SC1058244 RCAHMS

'DRAWING A NEW MAP OF LEARNING'
SPENCE AND THE UNIVERSITY OF SUSSEX

LOUISE CAMPBELL

The 1950s saw Spence established as a university architect. Appointed in March 1954 to draft a plan for the University of Edinburgh's central area, Spence produced in 1955 an outline for future development, which – although delayed and modified in response to pressure from the amenity societies – initiated the post-war expansion of the university. It led directly to several major jobs, notably his appointment as planner of the new science complex or 'Technopolis' at Nottingham, and as architect and planner of Southampton University. Southampton featured prominently in the architectural press as a turning-point in university design. The *Architectural Review* presented Spence's design for Southampton's science piazza as an elegant modern solution to the predicament of provincial redbrick universities, suffering from 'dim, stodgy and inappropriate accretions'.[1] Pressing for alternatives to what it termed the 'gratuitous monumentality' of recent building at Queen's University Belfast, the journal advocated compactness, bold planning and tall blocks. In its 1957 survey of the state of university architecture, Spence – alongside Hugh Casson, Leslie Martin,

William Holford and Basil Ward – was accorded the status of a pioneer.

The years 1957 and 1958 were pivotal ones for university design.[2] The expansion in university provision for science and technology generated work for Spence's Edinburgh and London offices; the universities of Liverpool and Newcastle as well as Southampton commissioned buildings to house newly appointed, cutting-edge scientists, their laboratories and equipment. In 1957–8 Cambridge University also began to embrace modern architecture. A small but prestigious commission to design a new residence for Queens' College was given to Spence, and the resulting publicity helped to reinforce his reputation as a moderniser and a conciliator, attractive to students, to alumni (who were paying half the cost of the new building) and to the College Fellows. Leslie Martin's arrival as professor at the School of Architecture in 1956 had encouraged a heightened awareness of contemporary architecture in Cambridge, spearheaded by the student Group for Architecture and Planning, who were vociferous in their condemnation of conservative new buildings. Like the celebrated Anti-Ugly Action group, who organised demonstrations against new buildings, Cambridge students began to target designs of which they disapproved.[3] Among these was a design by the traditionalist architect Stephen Dykes Bower for the residence at Queens', which they attacked for its historicist character.[4] Deeply offended, Dykes Bower withdrew from the job, leaving a vacancy for which Spence seemed an obvious choice on the strength of his recent work. Spence's design for Queens' was to be 'a test-case for modern architecture' in collegiate Cambridge.[5]

The new residence occupied a site on the Backs between the Fellows' garden and ancient bowling green, and the Victorian buildings of Friar's Court. The perspective reproduced in *The Times* in January 1958, showing a five-storey slab raised on columns, with a cylindrical stair-tower rising above the parapet of the roof terrace, caused a furore in the letters column.[6] Redesigned by December 1958 to a reduced height and with a different window arrangement, the new residence – known as the Erasmus Building – contained

116 View through the entrance arch of Falmer House, University of Sussex
SC1046612 RCAHMS

117 A proposal for the University of Edinburgh, *c*.1955
DP012579 RCAHMS

forty-three undergraduate study bedrooms and accommodation for two Fellows [**118**]. Reminiscent of a Corbusian housing slab, the Erasmus Building signalled an uncompromising modern approach to college accommodation while its columns and brick arches (designed to echo the brick arcade of adjacent Cloister Court), ensured that views between river and quad were retained. Le Corbusier's residence for Swiss students at the Cité Universitaire in Paris of 1930, raised above a gaunt undercroft, overlooked an athletics track and the city beyond. By contrast, the ground floor of Spence's building – accommodating the subtle change of levels between the Backs and the quad – instead provided a sheltered prospect of the bowling green and the river, and a paved terrace 'designed for use during May balls and other college occasions'.[7]

Queens' College paved the way for a more adventurous approach to university buildings at Cambridge, and later at Oxford.[8] It also helped to establish Spence's credentials as a modern architect. Conversely, however, the experience of a traditional college – the organisation of student rooms around a shared staircase, the spaces of the quadrangle and the college garden, the rituals of dining in hall and of chapel – was a formative one for him. In the 1960s, Spence went on to secure a series of commissions for university buildings in other historic cities, notably at Durham, Exeter and Edinburgh, where the university library was completed to the designs of his partners Hardie Glover and Andrew Merrylees in 1967. But it was the University of Sussex, and the blank sheet which its out-of-town setting provided, that most excited him, and which he regarded, with Coventry Cathedral, as his most personal work.

The University of Sussex enjoyed a head start among the seven new universities created in the 1960s, thanks to a vigorous local campaign to found a university at Brighton, and to an academic planning committee which rapidly worked out the organising principles for it and chose a vice-chancellor, John Fulton, a Balliol-trained philosopher.

Spence was apparently one of several architects who were approached in 1958.[9] His appointment, like that of Fulton, was announced in early 1959. Fulton's vision of the new University of Sussex was conceived in reaction both to the traditional Oxbridge model of collegiate life and to the civic or suburban university environment, drab in appearance and lacking social focus, which he had experienced at University College Swansea. The new academic structure

118 Erasmus Building, Queens' College, Cambridge, 1960
SC1048117 RCAHMS

planned at Sussex – comprising Schools of Studies rather than traditional departments – but remaining fluid before the first academic appointments were made, represented a considerable challenge for the designer. Fulton proposed that one of the first buildings of the university campus should be a social building which provided a place for students and staff to eat, to mix, to debate and to relax. This was seen as particularly important because at first there was no intention to build residential accommodation.[10] This social building, College House (re-named Falmer House in 1961), was conceived as performing a dual role, signalling a university which was determinedly non-collegial – or perhaps neo-collegial – in its structure, while providing students with a physical base and a sense of the institution during the chaotic period while teaching buildings were still under construction [**119**].

Fulton's desire to forge a distinctive 'Sussex *esprit*' and academic identity found a responsive echo in his architect.[11] Spence's description of Falmer House in terms of a gatehouse or grand entrance giving a foretaste of what lay beyond, and of a quadrangle, the classic format for an

119 Falmer House,
University of Sussex, 1962
SC1046627 RCAHMS

academic precinct, suggests his engagement with Fulton's ideas.[12] He also provided a lyrical account of the 200 acre site – a downland valley between Brighton and Lewes, with a line of mature trees running up the valley bottom: 'Rising from this emerald saucer are soft rolling hills decorated with casual clumps of trees between which one is afforded delicious glimpses of the surrounding downland country.'[13]

This landscape determined both the layout of the university campus and the architecture of the buildings. Spence chose to build low, allowing the trees to dominate the skyline, to use a soft red Sussex brick, and to centre the university around a pedestrian Great Court with buildings conceived in relation to the backdrop of the downs and to the screening effect of the existing trees. Considerations of contour and of planting were to inform Spence's subsequent

decisions about the planning of buildings, and he engaged the landscape architect Sylvia Crowe as adviser.[14]

At Southampton University, Spence had to cope with the problems of a pre-existing campus added to at intervals, whose growth was inhibited by the adjoining residential suburb.[15] Although there were precedents at Birmingham and Keele for laying out new buildings in parkland, there were simply no precedents in Britain for laying out a university from scratch on the scale of Sussex.[16] The Cranbrook Academy in Michigan and Aarhus University in Denmark provided Spence with two stimulating models of how this might be done. Cranbrook, designed by Eliel Saarinen, was visited by Spence in 1953 during a fund-raising trip to Canada undertaken for the Coventry Cathedral Reconstruction Committee; he described it as 'a Shangri-La of a university with porticoes, pools and fountains lavish with [Carl] Milles' sculpture, rich in flowers and with an art gallery'.[17] The character of Cranbrook's environment as a feast for the aesthete – well landscaped and richly endowed with art – helped to shape Spence's subsequent approach to university layout, beginning with the University of Edinburgh scheme of 1955, with its semi-enclosed spaces and sculpture [117]. Sussex, where the sciences were to be equally balanced by the arts (in contrast to the science and technical buildings which dominated Spence's university work in the late 1950s) encouraged him to think in these terms. So too did Fulton's view that education involved not merely intellectual formation, but social and cultural development as well. Aarhus University, despite being built over a long period (1935–47, and continued from the 1950s onwards) achieved a surprising degree of unity: 'the parts are complete in themselves' Spence noted.[18] The way in which the great window of the *aula* or hall and the curved, arcaded brick terrace beside it dominated the undulating site was perhaps also important.[19]

The format of Falmer House was evolved in 1959–60 by Spence in collaboration with his assistants and associates. The original idea of an academic quadrangle assumed a more urban and defensive character, the pastoral setting contrasting with the paving of the courtyard and the placing of a moat within its perimeter.[20] Flat concrete arches riding upon brick piers created a colonnade around the courtyard, with vaults of different spans and heights, interspersed with terrace voids. Spence likened this to 'four chests of drawers arranged around a square space with some of the drawers taken out'.[21] A triple-height vault, centrally placed, served as entrance portal. The staff common room and library were located on either side, wittily linked by a portcullis-like bridge [116]. On the south side of the courtyard, the giant windows of the student common room provided a corresponding echo, allowing students a commanding view of entrances and exits in the courtyard below and the campus beyond. The axis thus established was the organising principle of the campus core. Plans published in April 1960 show an open rectangular court occupying the valley-bottom north of Falmer House, bordered to the north by the arts building, to the west by a library, with a less formally grouped science enclave occupying an equivalent area on rising ground to the east.

Because of pressure to complete key buildings in time for the arrival of the first intake of students in 1962, Spence's

associate Gordon Collins and Povl Ahm of Ove Arup's devised a system involving the rapid on-site production of concrete vaults, columns and beams.[22] Around this slender framework were fitted brick walls and piers and curved concrete gable beams. The industrial character of this method of construction belied the monumental appearance of these buildings, with their massive vaults and robustly textured surfaces, designed to throw strong shadows, a language derived from Le Corbusier's late buildings.[23] The same architectural language of piers and arched concrete vaults was employed in the Physics Building [121], begun simultaneously, its structural system slightly modified to provide for different floor loading. Its façade – regular and solid in contrast to the arrangement of Falmer House – was designed as a giant colonnade, with projecting piers and a massive overhanging arcade. Based on the Stoa of Atticus in Athens (recently restored by American archaeologists), it presented a strikingly different image of science from that at Liverpool, Nottingham and Southampton.

This classical idiom permeated the core of the campus. Spence referred to the Athenian Agora, and also to the exposed brick arches of the Roman Colosseum in its ruined state.[24] These references echoed an important aspect of the educational programme at Sussex, where academics like Asa Briggs proposed multi-subject degree structures which would encourage breadth and inquisitiveness rather than narrow specialism. All arts undergraduates were required to take a philosophy course, and Briggs aimed to equip students to navigate what he described as a 'new map of learning' by giving them an understanding of the intellectual history of their subjects.[25] The Great Court was, like the Agora, dedicated to the exchange of ideas and the intellectual life of the community, providing a formal counterpart to Falmer House, designed for sociability and informal exchange.

The construction of the buildings which fringed this symbolic space occurred under more difficult circumstances than those which went before. The University Grants Committee (UGC) had made special allowance for Falmer House in recognition of the urgency of completing it and its special role as a flagship building.[26] Sussex's agreement to accelerate student intake to 3,000 by 1967–8 meant that the buildings of the second phase – arts, the library, chemistry and engineering – had to be larger than envisaged.[27] Spence's office came under pressure to produce new working drawings for these while keeping to strict cost limits. The first of these – the

120 Falmer House, University of Sussex, 1962
SC1066488 RCAHMS

121 Physics Building, University of Sussex, 1962
SC1046675 RCAHMS

122 Meeting House, University of Sussex, 1967
SC1046895 RCAHMS

123 Students' Common Room from the second floor balcony, Falmer House, University of Sussex, 1962
SC1046620 RCAHMS

124 Design for the Arts
Building and Library,
University of Sussex, 1961
DP014764 RCAHMS

library – managed to combine an imposing exterior, redolent of a great 'treasure house', with an interior of inviting accessibility.[28] The Arts Building with which Spence proposed to close the vista from Falmer House had a more difficult passage. Here, the spectacularly cantilevered lecture theatres, which were depicted sprouting from the base of two pylons at the entrance to the building, were ruled out by cost. More conventionally designed theatres took their place, but the H-shaped 'symbol of incompleteness' remained to mark the ceremonial centre of the campus; behind them, stepping up the slope, were lecturers' rooms arranged around quadrangles.[29]

Hugging the shoulders of the valley beside the physics block was the chemistry building, with a pair of semi-circular lecture theatres attached to its flank. This device – of using rounded forms to provide contrast with the harder shapes and staccato rhythms of light and shadow generated by the main buildings – informed developments in the mid- to late-1960s. Spence's plan of 1960 showed a free-standing hall, designed as a cylinder enclosed by a double tier of arcaded vaults, situated in the Great Court. However, Sussex (like Edinburgh and Southampton) decided quite early on to dispense with a great hall and to hold its ceremonies elsewhere. Some of the features of this concept informed the design of two subsequent buildings on the Sussex campus: a chapel and an arts centre. Paid for by benefactors, and thus

freer from the cost constraints which controlled the teaching buildings, they helped to enrich both the architectural character and the life of the campus. The chapel, located beside a long reflecting pool north-east of Falmer House, was at the university's insistence designated a non-denominational building, and re-named the Meeting House [**122, 125**]. A place of worship, a place for secular meetings, and providing the quiet spaces which had become increasingly scarce in Falmer House, the Meeting House proved an absorbing design task for Spence and Anthony Blee between 1963 and its completion in 1967. The Gardner Centre for the Arts supplied studio space and exposure to the visual and performing arts, which was deemed to be essential to an out-of-town campus.[30] Sited to the west of the Great Court, it contained an auditorium wrapped around with studios, performance rooms and a gallery, and provided a solid-walled foil to the pierced concrete rotunda of the Meeting House.

In order to concentrate on the completion of this central group, Spence brought in other architects to design a new refectory building and the halls of residence which the university had decided to build, but oversaw their designs in the capacity of consultant.[31] Meanwhile other new buildings for teaching and research, an administration building, and a second phase of the library were completed by his practice.

Spence's approach to Sussex was unashamedly driven by aesthetics. In interviews and lectures, he emphasised that it was the architecture and landscape which would unify the complex, rapidly evolving set of buildings which made up the university, rather than the quadrangular layout.[32] Running parallel with his choice of architectural forms of great simplicity and strength is an emphasis on a repertoire which included traditional materials like timber, brick, copper and flint. Spence suggested that the passage from school to university should be articulated in terms of a distinctive architectural environment. He recommended using glass and synthetic materials and finishes sparingly in order to avoid the excessive light and noise levels and the lightweight appearance characteristic of modern open-plan schools.[33] Two inter-related concepts of the university student of the 1960s emerge from his writing. The first is the shy school-leaver, needing the enclosure and reassurance of the quadrangle and cloister, and contemplative space. The second is a more boisterous individual, needing a robust architecture, capable of withstanding rough treatment, as a framework for activities, someone perhaps in need of civilising.[34] The University of Sussex – and Falmer House in particular – was conceived as an environment for both, a sort of social condenser evoking in its extraordinary spaces the egalitarian quality of the post-war university, mixing together the grammar school and public school product, the undergraduate and the lecturer, while its component elements – cloister, galleried refectory, pantry, debating chamber and common room – provide a faint echo of the rituals and the collegiate life which it replaced.[35]

Spence was not alone in aspiring to provide the university student with buildings of 'nobility', ones which would leave them with the 'feeling of having been cosseted in the architectural sense'.[36] Peter Chamberlain wrote in 1961 of creating an 'ennobling environment' and a visually rich and rewarding architecture.[37] Behind this rhetoric lay the desire to expunge the legacy of the red-brick university, and its perceived association with fustiness and bombast.[38] How better to do so than to re-invent university architecture either in terms of a cool rationalism or in terms of high drama and ceremony, of sculptural forms, thrilling spaces and handsome materials? Chamberlain Powell and Bon chose the former for Leeds University's plan and the latter for the court and hall of New Hall Cambridge in 1961.[39] Richard Sheppard Robson and Partners' buildings for Churchill College (a competition for which Spence acted as assessor in 1959), spearheaded a wave of monumental collegiate architecture at Cambridge and Oxford in the 1960s, featuring great concrete vaults and brick, superb finishes and a judicious use of flamboyant gestures.[40] It is unsurprising that the University of Sussex, founded by Oxford alumni and benefiting in its first two years from special treatment from the UGC, should approximate more closely to this mode of design than to that of the other new universities of the 1960s.

125 Interior of the Meeting House, University of Sussex
SC1042944 RCAHMS

THE ARCHITECT AND THE ARTISTS

PHILIP LONG

Basil Spence considered art to be an essential component of architecture. His desire for artistic collaboration reached its apogee in the building of Coventry Cathedral, where he employed not only specialists in stained and etched glass, letter cutting and mosaic, but also painters and sculptors of international repute such as Graham Sutherland and Jacob Epstein. As a celebration of progressive art and craft alone it remains exceptional in modern British architecture. Spence's interest in working with artists can be traced back to his youthful artistic ability. At Edinburgh College of Art, his first declared interest had been in sculpture before he decided to specialise in architecture.

At that time, in the late 1920s and through the 1930s, Edinburgh was associated with a string of talented painters and sculptors whom Spence was likely to have come into contact with at Edinburgh College of Art, first as a student and then as a tutor. His friendships with the sculptors Hew Lorimer and Thomas Whalen began when they met as students. Spence would later employ both, in particular Whalen, with whom he had a long professional relationship. He also maintained friendships with prominent Scottish or Scottish-born painters such as William Oliphant Hutchison, William Gillies, Anne Redpath, Robin Philipson, Alan Davie and William Scott, involving them in his projects or collecting their work. Particularly prized was a 1956 painting by Scott, *Brown Still Life*, acquired by Spence on its first exhibition, and subsequently recognised as a key work in the artist's oeuvre.

Spence's first commissions, predominantly for private houses, were in themselves strongly stated designs that appeared not to require further embellishment, even if budget had allowed. At Broughton Place, however, Hew Lorimer was asked to contribute carvings and ironwork, adding to the flavour of its historic style, which was to emulate that of Robert Lorimer, the sculptor's architect father. Spence's first opportunity to work fully in collaboration with artists was at the 1938 Glasgow Empire Exhibition. In the most progressive looking building on the site, Spence produced for ICI a futuristic structure largely constructed from the company's

own materials [see **52**]. Inside, in the upper gallery, the story of the company was told in the mural paintings of Donald Moodie and Robert Westwater, both of whom had studied and were now tutors at Edinburgh College of Art. On the outside Spence employed Whalen to produce sculptural reliefs for the pavilion's three distinctive triangular towers, the stylised forms of a tree, bird and fish repeating separately on each in representation of earth, air and water [**127**]. Under direction from the architect Thomas Tait, Spence also designed one of the two Scottish pavilions, the Scottish Pavilion North, which highlighted advancements made in Scottish public services. The entrance hall was dominated by Whalen's large figure entitled *Service*, which held a Torch of Knowledge in one hand and a Staff of Health in the other.

Is not clear to what extent Spence had a hand in the Scottish Pavilion interior displays; it is unlikely, for example, that he would have been particularly familiar with the work of Walter Pritchard, the Dundee born and trained stained-glass artist, who provided a mural. Throughout, the exhibition provided extensive opportunities for a diverse range of artists, introducing their work to a wide public as well as to design professionals. In a further building by Spence, an ideal modern Scottish house [see **145**], the Society of Scottish Artists was invited to hang a selection of paintings, including a number of landscape watercolours by William Gillies, a tutor at Edinburgh whom Spence knew and later acquired his work. A history of Scottish painting made up the principal contents of a further pavilion, the Palace of Art, but in the modern section Spence would have been able to see the work of other British artists, including that of Jacob Epstein, who he was later to commission at Coventry.

During the war Spence served as a camouflage officer, alongside the New Zealand-born artist John Hutton, who was to become an important contributor to the architect's post-war projects. After war service, architectural commissions were for some time scarce but Spence was able to pursue exhibition work, which culminated in designs for the nationwide 1951 Festival of Britain. In Glasgow, Spence was appointed Chief Architect of the Exhibition of Industrial

126 Jacob Epstein's sculpture *St Michael and the Devil* in progress in his studio, *c.*1957
SC1066339 RCAHMS

Power held in the Kelvin Hall, which was to celebrate Britain's contribution to heavy engineering. This was an apposite subject for a city whose wealth and reputation had been based on such industry, but which had been in sharp decline since the 1930s. Throughout the exhibition artists and designers were brought into play, contributing murals, engraved glass screens and sculpture to a series of theatrical displays laid out in a predetermined route. Entry to the exhibition was through the Hall of Power [**128**], a horseshoe-shaped chamber clad in a black relief by Whalen depicting the exhibition's themes, and described in the official guide as 'by far the biggest sculpture in Scotland'. On the far left of Whalen's work, a ruggedly modelled figure representing the God of Nature pointed to the beginning of a display on coal. Whalen's sculpture continued with figures of man, shown at work in coal seams. At the centrepoint was a doorway reached by a grand stairway, through which was a blazing light representing the sun.

Within the other halls, which were created by other designers and script-writers but under the overall control of Spence, appeared the work of other notable artists. The Polish born painter Aleksander Zyw, an émigré to Edinburgh in 1940, executed a mural telling the story of steam in a section devoted to Power and Industry. In the Hall of Shipbuilding and Railways was a mural by the English artist Michael Ayrton and a glass screen devoted to the engineer Richard Trevithick by John Hutton. Spence took design responsibility for the final spectacle in the exhibition, the Hall of the Future, which featured the work *Atomic Mural* by the former Glasgow School of Art and Léger student William Crosbie [**129**]. A number of studies exist for this (in the Sir Basil Spence Archive), in which Crosbie developed a vision depicting the as yet unknown beneficial aspects of atomic science to humankind. At the same time, Crosbie was at work elsewhere for Spence, on the design of a large mural for the entrance of Duncanrig School in East Kilbride, one of Spence's first post-war building commissions. This too was on the theme of life and industry.

One of the focal points of the 1951 Festival of Britain in London on the South Bank was Spence's Sea and Ships Pavilion [see p.57]. Its massive scale and use of a steel framework allowed the architect to create an innovative transparent structure reminiscent of constructivist sculpture. Within and around this could be incorporated exhibits and artworks alike, the latter used by Spence to convey more

127 Thomas Whalen's sculptural reliefs for the ICI Pavilion, Glasgow Empire Exhibition, 1938
SC1063853 RCAHMS

opposite

128 Spence's design for the Hall of Power, Exhibition of Industrial Power, Glasgow, 1951
DP018861 RCAHMS

129 William Crosbie's study for *Atomic Mural* for the Hall of the Future, for the Exhibition of Industrial Power, Glasgow, *c.*1950/1
DP012308 RCAHMS

FESTIVAL OF BRITAIN 1951 : EXHIBITION OF INDUSTRIAL POWER : THE SOURCES OF POWER HALL

general themes. Of the artworks, the largest was John Hutton's semi-abstract mural (thirty feet high by sixty feet wide) depicting man's involvement with the sea and his dependence on it. On the same elevation, and clearly seen from the north bank of the River Thames, was a vast sculptural group [130], *The Islanders*, by the Viennese born Siegfried Charoux, who had come to England in 1935. Showing a man, woman and child dressed in seafaring clothes and defiantly looking out, its production by an émigré who had found a home, and safety, in the British Isles must have added to its post-war symbolism of Britain as an island nation. Adjacent to the pavilion, and described in Spence's paperwork as part of the associated art works, was a tall water-activated mobile by Richard Huws, who had begun his career studying naval architecture before transferring his attention to sculpture. His work for the South Bank comprised of a forty-five foot high mast, to which were attached metal vanes, the movement of which was activated by water flowing from the top of the structure. Elsewhere in the pavilion Spence employed the sculptors Keith Godwin and Maurice Lambert and the painters Tristram Hillier, James Boswell and George Sholly, the latter three each executing murals.

As with the Empire Exhibition, the Festival of Britain on the South Bank, in addition to its wider aspirations, was an exposition of contemporary art. Artists were involved throughout the pavilions, while an exhibition of sculpture was held across the site. John Piper, who was to become involved at Coventry, produced a vast mural for the exterior of the Houses and Gardens Pavilion. Edward Bawden, who was later commissioned by Spence to provide a mural for the British Pavilion at Expo' 67, provided a work for the Lion and Unicorn Pavilion. Among the sculptors represented were two of Britain's most prominent: Jacob Epstein, with a piece entitled *Youth Advancing*, and Henry Moore with *Reclining Figure* of 1951.

Both these artists were receiving wider recognition, in particular Moore, who in the same year was the subject of a major retrospective at the Tate Gallery (one on Epstein was to be held in 1952). Such prolific evidence of their work was likely to have contributed to Spence's desire to involve Moore and Epstein at Coventry. Spence first visited the bomb-damaged site in the autumn of 1950. On the reverse of his copy of the competition's official conditions he made an outline sketch for the new cathedral and a note of the artists who at this early stage he presumably wished to involve. At

that time he was preoccupied with preparations for the festival and the names of Charoux, Lambert, Godwin and Huws appear, along with the English sculptors Frank Dobson and John Skeaping and earlier associates Whalen and Lorimer. Up to this point Spence had habitually re-employed artists he had previously worked with, but interestingly, with the exception of John Hutton, none received commissions for Coventry Cathedral. Winning the competition was of deep personal significance to Spence who as a student had produced exquisite drawings of medieval architecture and as an army intelligence officer in 1940 had reported the bombing of Coventry and the loss of its cathedral to his commanding officer. His submission to the competition (pronounced the winner in August 1951) did not include reference to specific artists, but from that point he began to formulate a precise selection, now informed by the extensive artistic talent evident from the Festival of Britain celebrations.

Spence showed the utmost devotion to the Coventry Cathedral project, even accompanying the cathedral authorities to Canada in 1953 on a fund-raising tour for its construction. From the moment his winning design was announced he found himself the subject of attention. Much of this was critical: to general opinion his vision did not pay sufficient homage to the historical forms it was replacing; to the design profession his plan was un-revolutionary. Spence openly addressed both through lectures and other appearances, and in his choice of artists put in place the sort of progressive elements that were felt to be lacking by many of his architectural peers.

This process was complicated, however. The rebuilding of the cathedral was a powerfully symbolic act of regeneration, and it became a subject of national and international interest and focus for conciliatory gesture. In the Chapel of Unity the marble mosaic floor by the prominent Swedish artist Einar Forseth, who had designed mosaics for Stockholm City Hall, came about through Forseth's personal enthusiasm to contribute after having visited the site. The cost was met through a subscription raised among the Swedish community and Forseth personally gifted a set of stained-glass windows for elsewhere in the cathedral [131]. The cost of English artist Margaret Tratherne's stained glass for the Chapel of Unity was also met from outside, through a donation from President Heuss of West Germany on behalf of the German Evangelical Churches. Spence consulted closely with the artists and the reconstruction committee over all

130 Sea and Ships Pavilion, showing the mural by John Hutton and the sculptural relief, *The Islanders*, by Siegfried Charoux, 1951
SC1046670 RCAHMS

131 Einar Forseth, stained-glass design for Coventry Cathedral, 1961
SC1030896 RCAHMS

132 Elisabeth Frink, bronze eagle lectern at Coventry Cathedral, 1962
SC1029691 RCAHMS

133 Ralph Beyer, 'I and the Father are One …', one of eight Tablets of the Word, which are installed in the nave recesses at Coventry Cathedral, 1962
SC1029715 RCAHMS

the commissioned designs, but as his and others' ambition for the building and its contents developed, so did criticism over the lack of involvement of Coventry-based contractors, artists and craftsmen. To some local eyes, the building was firstly the cathedral of Coventry rather than a national monument demanding national and international participation.

In his design description for the Chapel of Industry, Spence acknowledged that from the beginning, 'craftsmanship was to have a place in the Cathedral, for Coventry is predominantly an industrial town where craftsmen hold an honourable place'. A proposal was made that the chapel would display examples of the original cathedral's stained glass, but the dominating contribution was from Geoffrey Clarke, the Derbyshire-born artist, who produced a sculptural crown of thorns to be suspended in Spence's airy, glazed space [see 65]. Clarke contributed more designs than any other artist, including three of the nave windows, a cross [135] and candlesticks for the high altar as well as for the undercroft, and the flying cross for the *flèche*. As a student at the Royal College of Art, he had begun in graphic design, but soon became interested in working in a broader range of media, including stained glass and forged and welded iron. His adaptability must have appealed to Spence, as must have his progressive position; in 1951 he had produced a sideboard with the designer Robin Day, while in 1952 he was selected

for inclusion in the exhibition of young British sculptors at the Venice Biennale. He subsequently pioneered a method of casting aluminium sculptures from carved polystyrene models, and his flying cross was made using this technique.

At the same time as working on Coventry, Geoffrey Clarke was elsewhere employed by Spence's practice. In a 1956 preview of the Thorn Building in St Martin's Lane, published in the the *Architect's Journal*, it was noted that a sculpture was to be sited on the east wall, 'possibly by Eduardo Paolozzi'. Clarke produced the eventual work, known as the *Spirit of Electricity*. Forged and cast in bronze, this comprised of a seventy-seven foot high elongated curving form, with a concentration of protrusions and spikes at its centre. Clarke was further employed by the practice, designing the mosaic for Liverpool University's physics building and the external sculpture for a further physics building at Newcastle University. At Beaulieu, Spence's weekend home, a work by Clarke was sited in the garden [134].

Like Clarke, Elisabeth Frink was another young sculptor attracting critical attention in the mid–1950s. Both had been among the many who had made a submission to the international competition for a monument to the unknown political prisoner held in 1953; Frink's entry won a prize. From early on in her career she had made some sculpture which dealt with religious subjects, including, while still a student at Chelsea School of Art, a figure of *Christ at the Pillar*. From the beginning her sculpture had a prophetic, arcane quality which set it apart from the more overtly angular and constructed work of Clarke, Bernard Meadows, Reg Butler and other British contemporaries. For the lectern at Coventry Frink modelled an eagle [132], which was cast in bronze, as well as two emblems to be suspended above the clergy stalls: a mitre for the Bishop and a flame for the Provost, in beaten gilded copper. Although correspondence with the artist in Spence's files indicate there was some disagreement over the cost, Frink wrote to the architect that she 'was extremely pleased and proud to be asked to do these things'. A separate cast of the eagle was ordered for Spence's personal collection.

Frink's work was not completed until 1962, the year of the cathedral's consecration. Spence had begun devising the major artistic elements in the building shortly after winning the competition, conscious of the long negotiations that likely lay ahead. The lengthiest and most fraught was for the tapestry which the architect envisaged hanging the length of

134 Basil Spence's house, Beaulieu, with a sculpture by Geoffrey Clarke, *c.*1961
SC1048472 RCAHMS

the altar wall. Spence recounted the genesis of the work in his memoir, *Phoenix at Coventry*:

About the time the competition was announced, the Arts Council had held an exhibition of tapestries by famous British artists. The tapestries were all made by the Edinburgh Tapestry Company, owned by the Bute family. I had been struck by the brilliance of the colours and the non-reflective quality that tapestry has and I was particularly attracted to one of *Wading Birds* by Graham Sutherland. I have always admired his work and his painting of the Crucifixion at Northampton had made a deep impression on me. When I went to the old Coventry Cathedral for the first time I decided that a great tapestry, the height of the nave, should hang behind the altar, and that if I was successful in the competition, I would ask Graham Sutherland to design it and the Edinburgh Tapestry Company to weave it.

Spence visited Sutherland in France soon after winning the competition to begin negotiations (and acquired *Wading Birds* for his personal collection). Sutherland reacted cautiously, but eventually accepted the commission. Such a project was predisposed to problems, given the demanding scale, the technical challenge of its weaving, and alterations to the design necessitated by Sutherland's own struggles with the composition and Spence's modifications to the building. In the event it was not woven in Edinburgh but at Felletin, near Aubusson, in France and while nearing completion put an extraordinary strain on the relationship between architect and artist, as Spence attempted to contain costs and Sutherland became increasingly anxious during the final stages of the tapestry's production. The installed work broadly followed Spence's and the cathedral authorities' written instructions, for a large figure of Our Lord in glory supported by the twelve apostles, which Spence sketched out in his early studies of the interior. Spence and Sutherland agreed that the finished work would retain vitality if it was produced from a small-scale painted cartoon (just seven feet in height) provided by the artist. The completed tapestry was not seen in entirety until hung in the cathedral (an issue of particular contention to the artist, who wished to inspect the whole work prior to the final installation), and its transformation to such a vast scale (just over seventy-four feet high and thirty-eight feet wide) magnified and drew attention to the more awkward passages in Sutherland's design. Spence, although worn down by the difficulties surrounding the work, wrote to Sutherland that he considered it a triumph. He later admitted he had at first been disappointed, but that

135 Geoffrey Clarke, altar cross and candlesticks for Coventry Cathedral, c.1960
SC1029708 RCAHMS

136 The Coventry Cathedral clergy, dressed in the vestments designed by John Piper, process in front of Graham Sutherland's monumental tapestry
Private collection

his admiration for it had progressively grown.

Further debate was had over the provision of sculpture for the interior. The architectural brief had called for the provision of 'Hallowing Places' around the outer walls, with the suggestion that these might be shallow recesses where sculpture or stained glass would represent an activity of human life. Spence began discussion with Henry Moore, who, together with Epstein, he described as 'giants in the world of sculpture'. Moore was adamant that wall reliefs would not

work, and also convinced Spence that such sculpture for the exterior would be similarly problematic (Moore had recently designed a relief in brick for the Bowcentrum in Rotterdam, and was dissatisfied with the weak light the work received because of its orientation). The sites for the envisaged Hallowing Places were in the recesses of the nave walls, lit by stained glass designed by Lawrence Lee, Head of Stained Glass at the Royal College of Art, together with two of his recent graduates, Keith New and Geoffrey Clarke, whose work Spence had been introduced to as an external examiner at the college. Spence conceded that lighting in the adjacent spaces might have been problematic and an alternative was devised – large stone tablets engraved with inscriptions and symbols [133]. These were undertaken by the sculptor and letter-cutter Ralph Beyer, who, in 1937, had escaped Nazi Germany and had come to study under Eric Gill. Beyer undertook further lettering work, including the massive floor inscription of bronze inlaid letters at the cathedral entrance.

For the exterior figure of St Michael, which was to be installed by the cathedral porch adjacent to the baptistery window, Spence approached Epstein. The architect had been impressed by the artist's recently unveiled *Madonna and Child* in Cavendish Square, close to Spence's new London offices. With that work, Epstein had succeeded in making a rounded figure sculpture that was hung on the flat without any visible support or attempt at framing. Epstein's reputation (and indeed his Jewish religion) meant his appointment was problematic for the cathedral authorities, but with the encouragement of the Bishop of Coventry, who had been deeply impressed by the spirituality of the Cavendish Square work, the commission was agreed. *St Michael and the Devil* was to be in the region of seventeen feet high, demanding that it was made in sections [126]. Epstein did not see the entire work assembled until it was in the foundry, and died prior to the unveiling in 1960, two years before the cathedral itself was opened [137]. The complex form of St Michael,

137 The south wall of Coventry Cathedral, during construction, and after the installation of the sculpture of *St Michael and the Devil* by Jacob Epstein, 1960
SC1029592 RCAHMS

138 Coventry Cathedral baptistery window, with stained glass by John Piper
Private collection

139 Crown of thorns screen designed by Basil Spence for the Gethsemane Chapel, Coventry Cathedral, 1961
SC1029628 RCAHMS

140 Canopy for the bishop's throne designed by Basil Spence and Anthony Blee, Coventry Cathedral, 1961
SC1029692 RCAHMS

with spread wings and arms out-held, standing over the conquered and monstrous devil, adds a dynamism to the plain exterior and was judged one of the most successful elements of the building. A unique cast of the head (modelled on Wynne Godley, the husband of Epstein's daughter Kitty) was produced at the same time for Spence, who also sat to Epstein for a portrait bust commissioned by the Royal Institute of British Architects, of which he was then president.

After seeing the figure of St Michael, the visitor would enter the new cathedral via the porch and then turn to face the fully glazed west elevation. Spence's idea for a clear glass screen the full height of the nave provided a continuum between the ruins of the old cathedral and the new, and for this he approached his previous collaborator John Hutton. The artist worked as a mural painter before coming to glass engraving: 'more or less by accident … It was from the point of view of a mural painter that I designed the engraving on the Great West Screen of Coventry Cathedral'. Hutton's previous glass designs (he had by then received several commissions

for war memorials) had been too 'tightly drawn' for Spence's requirements, and Hutton worked to produce a more spontaneous effect, which suited the ethereal subject matter of layers of angels and saints rising up through the full height of the great glass screen [see **70**].

The window proposed for the baptistery was of equal significance to Spence, as it was the only one that could be seen after passing through Hutton's screen. Its scale was substantial (with 198 lights), but the final decision to appoint John Piper, together with his collaborator Patrick Reyntiens, was not taken until 1957. As an official war artist Piper had made sketches in the ruins of Coventry Cathedral on the morning after it had been destroyed (the resultant painting was his first of bomb damage). His Festival of Britain mural would have been known to Spence, but he had not occurred as a stained glass artist until the architect's attention was drawn to the windows Piper designed in 1954 for Oundle School Chapel in Northamptonshire (Piper's first in that medium). Just prior to receiving the formal commission for Coventry, Piper visited Le Corbusier's Ronchamp Chapel, and saw the glass by Léger at Audincourt. The latter, as with Piper's designs for Oundle, was figurative, but at Coventry the density of the mullions suggested an abstract design. In the completed window the richly coloured glass gradually dissolves in the centre into a large circular form of brilliant golden yellow.

From the 1940s onwards Piper had worked as a set and costume designer. As he executed the cartoons for the baptistery glass he was consulted on the colour and form of the Coventry clergy vestments, and produced a number of striking designs of simplicity which stemmed from his pre-war abstract paintings and collages. The movement of a clerical procession through the nave, past Piper's window and dressed in the artist's bold appliquéd designs, progressing towards the sanctuary lit by the German refugee artist Hans Coper's statuesque candle holders, must have fulfilled Spence's vision of a plain casket adorned with jewels [**136**]. Despite the diversity of makers, the impression created is not one of disharmony, but of a unified design, within which beat the differing pulses of numerous creative talents. Sutherland's dominating tapestry may have directed that all other elements contained within the open expanse of the nave were abstract in form. However, for the separate Gethsemane Chapel, the cathedral's most jewel-like space, the artist Stephen Sykes (who had taught stained glass at Edinburgh College of Art) produced panels showing an angel and disciples, elaborately encrusted with glass, mirror and mosaic [see **77**]. This small chapel's concentrated drama is reinforced by Spence's own wrought iron crown of thorns screen [**139**]. While Spence has been referred to throughout this chapter as an orchestrator of artists, his own contribution and that of his architect-partner Anthony Blee to details within the cathedral must also be recognised. These were numerous and included, for example, the choir stalls surmounted by canopies of a geometric design reminiscent of thorns, which had been inspired by an elaborate frame Spence saw in the home of Graham Sutherland [**140**].

After the cathedral's consecration, Spence remained involved in discussions over proposed art works. Correspondence continued with Moore, but in spite of Spence's great enthusiasm for his art, opportunities for fruitful collaboration never greatly developed. A work was not found for Coventry, and while Spence was enthusiastically involved in discussions over a piece lent by Moore to the University of Sussex, the architect's proposal for a major

work to be situated in the pool at the front of the British Embassy, Rome, was lost as costs were cut. At Expo '67 however, Spence was able to arrange for the sculptor's *Locking Piece* to be sited within a pool at the front of the architect's British Pavilion [see **63**]. This also featured a sculptural fountain by Stephen Sykes, made of moulded fibreglass and multi-coloured mirror glass [**141**].

Throughout the 1960s and until the end of his career Spence continued to work with artists. Although the projects

141 Stephen Sykes, model for a fountain for the British Pavilion, Expo '67, Montreal
SC1047368 RCAHMS

he designed were substantial and prestigious, none offered the potential for artistic collaboration to the extent that the Festival of Britain or Coventry had provided, which had been substantial manifestations of the broader regenerative cultured spirit of the 1950s. Spence, however, had come to be known as an architect who cared about artists and about artistic detail, and his practice files are thick with letters from practitioners keen to draw their work to his attention or ask for his support. He remained precise in his choice of those he worked with, carefully matching artist and aesthetic with a locale and context that would be appropriate for their work. In this way, Spence identified a large 1960 canvas, *Day's Rest, Day's Work*, by Ivon Hitchens – primarily a landscape painter – for the refectory within the main building at the University of Sussex, which was set within the rural location of the South Downs [142]. For the restaurant at Glasgow Airport, the Scottish artist Robin Philipson produced a mural full of dynamic forms that suited the mood of this new building-type [143]. In Edinburgh, Anne Redpath was commissioned to produce a tapestry for the St Andrew Square board room of the solid and dependable firm of Scottish Widows. Writing to the General Manager as the building was completed, and ever mindful of his client's interests, Spence concluded: 'Personally, I think it is a little beauty and what is more, an investment!'

142 The refectory, Falmer House, University of Sussex, showing *Day's Rest, Day's Work* by Ivon Hitchens
SC1046618 RCAHMS

143 The restaurant, Glasgow Airport, showing the mural by Robin Philipson
SC988328 RCAHMS

CHRONOLOGY

NEIL GREGORY

Unless specified, the building projects selected for this chronology are shown in italics under the year in which they were completed or opened.

1907

Basil Urwin Spence born in Bombay on 13 August. Father, Urwin Archibald Spence, an analytical chemist, was assayer at HM Mint. Mother, Daisy Crisp.

1919–25

Attended George Watson's College, Edinburgh.

1925

Enroled at Edinburgh College of Art.

1926

Opted to study in the School of Architecture after first year of general art studies.

1928

Received his Architecture Certificate.

Awarded Royal Incorporation of Architects in Scotland (RIAS) prize for third year students.

1929

Spent a year in Sir Edwin Lutyens's office in London, assisting him with designs for Viceroy's House, New Delhi. Attended evening classes at the Bartlett School of Architecture under Professor A.E. Richardson.

1930

Returned to Edinburgh for final year of study. Appointed temporary junior assistant instructor in Design at ECA.

1931

Gained his Architectural Diploma.

Awarded Rowand Anderson medal by RIAS. Awarded Recognised Schools Silver Medal by Royal Institute of British Architects (RIBA) for best architecture student in Britain.

Received honourable mention from RIBA for his Pugin Travelling Studentship entry.

Formed architectural partnership Kininmonth & Spence, at 16 Rutland Square, Edinburgh.

1932

Awarded RIBA Arthur Cates prize for town planning, with Robert Matthew.

Appointed assistant instructor at ECA (until 1936).

144 Entrance to the Scottish Industries Exhibition, Kelvin Hall, Glasgow, 1949
SC1030879 RCAHMS

145 House for the Council for Art & Industry, Empire Exhibition, Glasgow, 1938
SC1054244 RCAHMS

1933

Awarded RIBA Pugin Travelling Studentship for sketches and measured drawings of Gothic architecture.

Elected Associate of RIBA.

1934

Married Mary Joan Ferris. Honeymoon in Germany.

Kininmonth & Spence absorbed into the Rowand Anderson practice, with both men becoming partners in the renamed Rowand Anderson & Paul & Partners firm.

Lismhor, Easter Belmont Road, Corstorphine, Edinburgh: one of a series of modernist villas commissioned from Kininmouth & Spence during the 1930s.

First commercial commission: *Southern Motors' Garage, Causewayside, Edinburgh.*

Began work as a designer of exhibitions: *Edinburgh Architectural Association display, Waverley Exhibition Centre, Edinburgh.*

1935

Lecturer in Advanced History at ECA (until October 1939).

1936

Cleghorn's shop, 129 Princes Street, Edinburgh.

First overseas commission: *Scottish Pavilion at the Empire Exhibition, Johannesburg.*

1937

First competition win: *Scottish School of Art & Industry, Kilsyth, Stirlingshire* begun in late 1930s and completed in 1954, inaugurating a series of school commissions on both sides of the border after the Second World War.

Visited Exposition Internationale des Arts et Techniques dans la Vie Moderne, Paris.

1938

Broughton Place, Peeblesshire.

Kininmonth & Spence became sole partners of Rowand Anderson & Paul & Partners.

Empire Exhibition, Glasgow: Imperial Chemical Industries (ICI) Pavilion: house for the Council for Art & Industry; Scottish Pavilions, the last in conjunction with Thomas Tait.

Quothquhan, near Biggar, Lanarkshire.

1939

Gribloch, Kippen, Stirlingshire (with Perry Duncan).

Commissioned as 2nd Lieutenant served with the Camouflage Training Development Unit, Farnham, Surrey, subsequently acting captain in Intelligence.

1940

Coventry Cathedral partially destroyed during air raid on 14 November.

1944

Landed in Normandy with the 3rd Infantry Division

1945

Demobilised from military duties in September. Mentioned twice in dispatches.

Returned to work at Rowand Anderson & Paul & Partners.

Received his first post-war local authority housing commission: Bannerfield estate, Selkirk.

1946

Established Basil Spence & Partners with Bruce Robertson, staff mostly drawn from Rowand Anderson & Paul & Partners, and promising students from ECA (Hardie Glover and Peter Ferguson).

Chief Architect for two exhibitions: *Chemistry At Your Service* and *Britain Can Make It, London.*

1947

Elected Fellow of RIBA.

Chief Architect of *Enterprise Scotland* exhibition, held during the first Edinburgh Festival.

Adviser to Board of Trade for British Industries Fair, until 1949.

First university commission: Natural Philosophy building, University of Glasgow, completed 1959.

1948

Awarded OBE, mainly in recognition of his work as an exhibition designer.

1949

Scottish Industries Exhibition, Kelvin Hall, Glasgow.

1951

London office established at Buckingham Street. *Festival of Britain:* Chief Architect of *Exhibition of Industrial Power, Kelvin Hall, Glasgow* and architect of *Sea and Ships Pavilion, South Bank, London.*

Received Festival of Britain award for housing at Sunbury, Middlesex.

Announced as winner of the Coventry Cathedral competition.

1952

London office moved to 48 Queen Anne Street. Elected to the RIBA Council and Associate of the Royal Scottish Academy (ARSA). Elected Associate of the Royal Academy (ARA).

Received Saltire Award for local authority housing at Dunbar, East Lothian.

1953

Moved home from Edinburgh to Queen Anne Street.

Embarked on a four-month fund-raising tour of Canada for Coventry Cathedral.

1954

Appointed Vice -President of RIBA (until 1955).

Appointed consultant architect for the University of Edinburgh's redevelopment of the George Square area, (for six years).

1955

Appointed Hoffman Wood Professor of Architecture, University of Leeds.

Appointed architect to Nottingham University Science Campus (master plan and eleven buildings), the first of three major university campuses in England.

1956

Appointed Honorary Secretary of RIBA (in 1956 only). Appointed member of the Royal Fine Art Commission (until 1970).

Appointed architect to Southampton University, master plan for Highfield Campus and nineteen buildings.

Visited the Chapel of Ronchamp and modern churches in France and Switzerland.

Sydenham County Secondary School, London.

Moved home to the new Spence office at 1 Canonbury Place, London.

1957

First parish churches in England and Scotland: *St Chad's Wood End; St Oswald's, Tile Hill; and St John the Divine, Willenhall; all in Coventry.*

St Andrew's Parish Church, Clermiston, Edinburgh.

1958

Appointed architect for Hampstead Civic Centre (Swiss Cottage), London.

Elected President of RIBA (for two years).

1959

Toured Africa in presidential capacity. Elected Honorary member of Institute of South African Architects, East Africa Institute of Architects and Ghana Society of Architects. Elected Honorary Fellow of American Institute of Architects and Honorary Corresponding Member of the Royal Architectural Institute of Canada.

Received commissions for the Chancery of the British Embassy in Rome and Hyde Park Cavalry Barracks, London.

Assessor, competition for the Liverpool Metropolitan (RC) Cathedral.

Assessor, competition for Churchill College, Cambridge.

Thorn House office block, London.

St Paul's Church, Ecclesfield, Sheffield; St Catherine's Church, Woodthorpe, Sheffield.

1960

Awarded knighthood. Elected Royal Designer for Industry (Exhibitions and Interiors) by the Royal Society of Arts.

Elected a Royal Academician.

President of the Building Centre Trust (until 1968).

1961

Opened an additional office at 1 Fitzroy Square, London.

Spence house, Beaulieu, Hampshire.

Professor of Architecture at the RA (until 1968).

1962

Received the Order of Merit.

Elected Honorary Fellow of the Royal College of Art and Treasurer of the RA (until 1964).

Phoenix at Coventry is published.

Coventry Cathedral consecrated on 25 May.

Falmer House opened, first of seventeen buildings Spence's practices designed at *the University of Sussex.*

Scottish Widows headquarters, St Andrew Square, Edinburgh.

1963

Received honorary degrees from Universities of Leicester and Manitoba, Canada.

1964

Three practices in operation: Sir Basil Spence OM RA at Canonbury; Sir Basil Spence Bonnington & Collins (Fitzroy Square, London), and Sir Basil Spence Glover & Ferguson (Edinburgh).

Served on the Arts & Architecture Committee for the John F. Kennedy Memorial Library, Cambridge, Massachusetts.

Bañalbufar, Majorca.

1965

Hutchesontown C Development, Queen Elizabeth Square, Gorbals, Glasgow.

1966

Abbotsinch (Glasgow) Airport opened by Queen Elizabeth II.

1967

Board of Trustees of the Civic Trust (until 1972).

left to right:

146 ICI Exhibition Stand, British Industries Fair, Olympia, London, 1948

147 Thorn House, Upper St Martin's Lane, Westminster, London

148 'The Beehive', extension to Parliament House, Wellington, New Zealand

149 Abbotsinch (Glasgow) Airport

150 E Building, Palais des Nations, Geneva, Switzerland

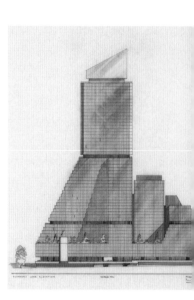

Mortonhall Crematorium, Edinburgh.

British Pavilion, Expo' 67, Montreal.

St Matthew's Church, Reading.

1968

Civic Trust Award for Crookfur Cottages, Newton Mearns.

RIBA Award for University of Edinburgh Main Library.

1969

Canongate Housing, Edinburgh.

Civic Trust Award for Sussex University Meeting House

1970

Civic Trust Award for the restoration of 100 Park Lane, London.

Received Coventry Award of Merit.

Hyde Park Cavalry Barracks, London.

Exhibition Hall and Boat House, Carmel College, South Oxfordshire.

1971

Dar Tal Ghar, Fawwara, Malta.

British Embassy, Rome, Italy.

1973

Honorary Member of the Academia di San Luca, Rome.

Extension to the Palais des Nations building, home of the United Nations Office, Geneva. (Appointed to building committee in 1964).

1975

Received the Grande Médaille d'Or, from the Académie d'Architecture, Paris.

1976

Scottish Widows HQ, Dalkeith Road, Edinburgh.

Bank of Piraeus, Athens.

Queen Anne's Gate offices, London (first proposed in 1964).

Worked on Bahrain Cultural Centre competition at his home Yaxley Hall, Suffolk whilst in respite from illness.

Died at Yaxley Hall, 19 November. Buried at St Mary's church-yard, Thornham Parva, Suffolk.

1977

Parliament extension, Wellington, New Zealand officially opened by Queen Elizabeth II (Spence acted as consultant to NZ Government from 1964 onwards).

Ionian and Popular Bank, Piraeus, Greece.

Kensington and Chelsea Town Hall, London.

Mariposa apartments, Cannes, France.

1978

A memorial inscription to Spence unveiled at Coventry Cathedral.

left to right:

151 Early sketch design for Queen Anne's Gate, London

152 Queen Anne's Gate, London

153 Project Z, an unexecuted scheme for a headquarters for a mining consortium, Collins Street, Melbourne, Australia

SOURCES

The principal source for documentary material relating to the design work of Basil Spence is the Sir Basil Spence Archive held within the collections of the Royal Commission on the Ancient and Historical Monuments of Scotland. It is available for public consultation at the RCAHMS Library, 16 Bernard Terrace, Edinburgh EH8 9NX and through its website: www.rcahms.gov.uk

The archive contains over 40,000 drawings, photographs, manuscripts and models relating to Spence's career as well as personal items including diaries, letters and sketches. The archive complements other Spence-related material held at RCAHMS, including 14,400 drawings and photographs from Spence's Scottish office (the Spence Glover & Ferguson Collection) that were catalogued in 2000 as part of the Heritage Lottery Funded Scottish Architects' Papers Preservation Project.

Other Sources

Berthoud 1982
Roger Berthoud, *Graham Sutherland*, London, 1982

Berthoud 1987
Roger Berthoud, *The Life of Henry Moore*, The Pallas Gallery, London, 1987

Black 1950
Misha Black (ed.), *Exhibition Design*, London, 1950

Bliss 1979
Douglas Percy Bliss, *Edward Bawden*, Godalming, 1979

Brawne 1967
Michael Brawne, *University Planning and Design, A Symposium*, Architectural Association paper no.3, London, 1967

Bullock 2002
Nicholas Bullock, *Building the Post-War World: modern architecture and reconstruction in Britain*, London, 2002

Campbell 1987
Louise Campbell, *To Build a Cathedral*, University of Warwick, 1987

Campbell 1996
Louise Campbell, *Coventry Cathedral: Art and Architecture in Postwar Britain*, Oxford, 1996

Daiches 1964
David Daiches (ed.), *The Idea of a New University: An Experiment in Sussex*, London, 1964

Donat 1965
John Donat, 'Sir Basil Spence on his work', *The Listener*, 2 February 1965

Edwards 1995
Brian Edwards, *Basil Spence 1970–76*, Edinburgh, 1995

Frink 1984
Elisabeth Frink: A Sculptural Catalogue Raisonné, Salisbury, 1984

Gardiner 1992
Stephen Gardiner, *Epstein*, London, 1992

Glendinning and Muthesius 1994
Miles Glendinning and Stefan Muthesius, *Tower Block*, London, 1994

Hitchens 1963
Ivon Hitchens, Tate Gallery, London, 1963

Hutton 1969
John Hutton, *Engraved Glass, Drawings, Paintings*, Commonwealth Institute Gallery, London, 1969

Lilley 1994
Clare Lilley, *Geoffrey Clarke RA*, West Bretton, 1994

McKean 1987
Charles McKean, *The Scottish Thirties: an Architectural Introduction*, Edinburgh, 1987

Maguire 1996
Robert Maguire, 'Continuity and Modernity in the Holy Place', *Architectural History*, vol. 39, 1996

Mills 1958
Edward Mills, 'Cathedral and churches by Basil Spence', *Architect and Building News*, 21 May 1958

Muthesius 2001
Stefan Muthesius, *The Postwar University: Utopianist Campus and College*, New Haven and London, 2001

Piper 1983
John Piper, Tate Gallery, London, 1983

Révai 1964
Andrew Révai (ed.), *Sutherland: The Coventry Tapestry*, London, 1964

Spence 1956
Basil Spence, 'The Modern Church', *RIBA Journal*, July 1956

Spence 1962
Basil Spence, *Phoenix at Coventry*, London, 1962

NOTES & REFERENCES

Evolution of a Practice Jane Thomas
pages 23–33

1 In 1949, Spence was ambitious and, like many architects at the time, getting frustrated with the lack of opportunity at home. He was impatient and remembers thinking, 'I had to get on, I had to get on.' At about this time, he considered going to the USA to work for Frank Lloyd Wright. See Donat 1965.
2 *House and Garden*, September 1954, pp.53–5.
3 According to Spence,'My parents were very poor, and I had one year (at Edinburgh College of Art) my mother had saved up sufficient … after that I was on my own'. See Donat 1965.
4 Edinburgh College of Art Report by the Board of Management to the Governors for the Session, 1925–6, pp.11–24 (continued for the next session 1927/8).
5 See Donat 1965.
6 According to Spence:'As my life is architecture, it is natural that part of my home is given over to studios where some of the projects in their formatic stages develop, and after a whole day at the RIBA I can go round the boards when all is quiet and see how things are going. I still draw and I try to reserve the weekends to this; in fact if I had not been asked to write these few words I would be on my drawing board'. *Architects Journal*, 21 January 1960, pp.103–4.
7 'But so much of my work seems to me to come from convincing people that my plans are good. I love selling'. 'Nancy Spain goes Visiting', *Woman*, 17 November 1962.
8 See Donat 1965.
9 'Says one of Spence's young men, despite the firm's expansion, it is still very much of a pyramid, with Basil Spence, the inspirer of his teams, the fount of ideas at the top. Despite its volume, all the firm's work carries his personal signature and is 'completely Spence' *Architecture and Design,* April 1959.
10 Richard Sheppard's obituary in *RIBA Journal,* vol.84, January 1977 on Spence's RIBA Presidency 'those two years were the most adventurous and inspiring I can remember in all the spells I served on the Council. This was entirely due to his personal qualities as a man and to his conception of the role of the architect'. Of meetings 'there was always a sense of drama, tension and excitement'. 'He lobbied Royalty, Ministers' departments, even the media and for a time the country was aware that architecture was important and absorbing.'

11 'The architect is a servant, a tailor, who cuts and measures the thin chap or the fat chap and tries to make him comfortable.' *The Guardian*, 21 October 1970.
12 Transcript of Spence's Founders Day Speech, George Watson's College, 1963. Sir Basil Spence Archive, NMRS reference MS2329/x/19/20.

First Buildings 1932–9 Clive B. Fenton
pages 35–47

1 Coincidentally, John Begg was serving in Bombay as government architect when Spence was born there in 1907.
2 John Summerson, 'Modernity in Architecture. An appeal for the new style', *The Scotsman*, 21 February 1930, p.8.
3 Ibid., subsequent letters, William Davidson (historian), *The Scotsman,* 27 February 1930; C d'O Pilkington Jackson (sculptor), *The Scotsman ,* 24 February 1930; J. Summerson, 28 February.
4 Kininmonth was articled to William H. Thomson in 1921 and attended part-time classes at ECA. The final two years, 1927–9, were spent as a full-time student. He was an assistant at Rowand Anderson & Paul from 1925–7 and 1930–1.
5 Sir William Kininmonth interviewed by Anthony Blee (January 1980) recording. Sir Basil Spence Archive, RCAHMS.
6 'House at Craiglockhart for Dr and Mrs Allan', Spence's perspective, is in the collection of Mr and Mrs Blee. Building consent was granted in June 1931, probably before Kininmonth & Spence was set up – Edinburgh City Archive.
7 Rowand Anderson ledgers. Private Collection, Edinburgh.
8 Spence's involvement is not known but an isometric drawing, by Kininmonth, which was exhibited at the Royal Scottish Academy in 1934 is in a private collection.
9 *Architect & Building News*, 9 August 1935. Building consent was sought in June 1933.
10 The roof terrace disappeared in 1948 when Kininmonth provided an extension at first floor level – Edinburgh City Archive.
11 White Cottage, 6 Comiston Rise, Edinburgh.
12 Drawings in the Sir Basil Spence Archive, RCAHMS are dated June 1939.
13 The practice was founded by Sir Robert Rowand Anderson (1834–1921) in 1891.

154 Sea and Ships Pavilion, Festival of Britain, London, 1951
SC102251 RCAHMS

14 Building consent for Cleghorn's, 129 Princes Street was sought in February 1936. Dean of Guild drawings in Edinburgh City Archive. Perspective drawings in RIAS collection at RCAHMS.

The Gourmenia, designed by Leo Nachlicht, which also had circular roof lights, was featured in the *Architectural Review,* 1930, p.129. Interestingly, Spence was able to achieve the cylindrical lift and spiral stair motif at the Scottish Widows building, St Andrew Square, Edinburgh (completed in 1962).

15 Transcript of interview with Kininmonth for the '1930s Survey' by the RIAS. RIAS Archive, Edinburgh.

16 At this time James Macgregor was Head of Architecture and Gleave was senior lecturer. Kininmonth's sister-in-law was also engaged to Gleave.

17 Broughton Place – Elliot Papers, in the RCAHMS.

18 'Tradition in Scottish Architecture', Basil Spence, *Building Industries,* April 1939.

19 Gribloch Papers in the RCAHMS.

20 The architects for the lodge were Copland & Blakey, of Falkirk. C. A. Macgregor states that the Falkirk firm were hired by Colville on the strength of a bungalow they built at Bannockburn, whereas C. McKean claims that the Bannockburn house was a copy of Gribloch. C. A. Macgregor 'Gribloch a 1930s Scottish Country House' in *Architectural Heritage* ,V, 1995, p.75. McKean 1987, p155–6. Whichever is the case, the executed lodge is similar to a rough perspective by Spence, dated December 1937, in the RIAS Collection, RCAHMS.

Exhibition Design Brian Edwards
pages 49–61

1 Basil Spence, 'Construction methods and materials' in Black 1950, p.113.

2 Ibid., p.106.

3 Here and elsewhere the author is indebted to Clive Fenton and David Walker's research as part of the ARHC Project, 'The Life and Work of Sir Basil Spence 1907–1976: Architecture, Tradition and Modernity'.

4 Besides recommending Spence along with three other architects to participate in a limited competition, Thomas Tait endorsed Spence's nomination for election to the RIBA that year.

5 Sidney Rogerson, 'Glasgow: ICI at the Exhibition', *ICI Magazine,* May 1938, p.394.

6 McKean 1987, p.38.

7 In 1936 office records at Balfour Paul show Spence earned £105 for the design of the Scottish Pavilion, which almost equalled that for Quothquhan, a nine-bedroom country house.

8 Spence in Black 1950, p.114.

9 Black 1950, p.27. See also *The Glasgow Herald,* 27 December 1948.

10 Black 1950, p.53.

11 Black 1950, pl.156.

12 Black 1950, pp.67–8.

13 José Manser, *Hugh Casson: A Biography*, New York, 2000, pp. 120–48.

14 Interview conducted with Sir Hugh Casson by Bruce Yoell, 7 November 1979.

15 Erik Mattie, *World's Fairs*, New York, 1998, p.228.

16 Sir Basil Spence Archive, RCAHMS, 172/26–30. Letter Central Office of Information (COI) to Spence dated 30 June 1964.

17 Sir Basil Spence Archive, RCAHMS, 172/26–30. Spence to COI, letter dated 1 June 1965.

18 Ibid.

19 Sir Basil Spence Archive, RCAHMS, 172/26–30. COI Design Panel Minutes, 29 October 1965.

20 Ibid.

21 Spence's lecture is reported at length in *The Montreal Star,* 16 October 1965.

22 Ibid.

23 *The Gazette,* 16 October 1965.

24 *The Montreal Star,* 16 October 1965.

25 *Daily Express*, 21 September 1966.

26 *Le Petit Journal*, 24 October 1965.

27 Peter Collins, *Changing Ideals in Modern Architecture*, London, 1965, p.287.

Shaping the Sacred Louise Campbell
pages 63–75

1 Elain Harwood, 'Public acclaim and critical disdain: the fall and rise of Coventry Cathedral', *Church Building*, vol.71, September/October 2001, p.40.

2 Basil Spence, 'The Cathedral Church of St Michael Coventry', *RIBA Journal*, February 1955, p.151.

3 See Alan Powers, 'The Expression of Levity', *Twentieth Century Architecture*, vol.5 (Festival of Britain), 2001, pp.49–56.

4 Food rationing continued until 1954; the Korean War began in 1950.

5 Spence's competition design proposed transplanting this altar into the new cathedral, where it would be placed beneath a tapestry depicting the crucified Christ. For a full account, see Campbell 1996, pp.54–9.

6 Howard Robertson, 'The Inaugural Address by the President', *RIBA Journal*, November 1952, p.4.

7 David Eccles, 'Coventry Cathedral: Minister's Reasons for Issuing a Building Licence', *Builder*, 30 April 1954, p.756. The letter, sent to Coventry City Council, was simultaneously released to the press.

8 *Coventry Cathedral: Architectural Competition Conditions and Instructions to Competing Architects*, October 1950, quoted in Spence 1962, p.4.

9 Spence 1962, pp.43–4. Ernest Ford, Chairman of the building [Reconstruction] Committee, commented on the revised layout of late 1951: 'It is wrong aes-

thetically, practically, psychologically and traditionally'. See Campbell 1996, p.92.

10 For the architecture of St Paul's, see Maguire1996, pp.1–18; and for its patron Father Gresham Kirby see Obituary, *Independent*, 22 August 2006.

11 Caroline van Eck, 'Piercing the rhetoric of form: an essay in architectural rhetoric', paper given at Art & Christianity Enquiry Conference, London, February 2001.

12 Memorandum enclosed in letter from Spence to Provost Williams, 25 May 1960, Sir Basil Spence Archive, RCAHMS.

13 Letter from Spence to Williams, ibid.

14 See R. Maguire letter to *Architects' Journal*, 11 April 1957 reproduced in Maguire 1996, pp.1–2 and Peter Hammond, 'A Liturgical Brief', *Architectural Review*, April 1958, pp.243–55. Spence had a different conception of function, writing in 1956: 'That elusive thing called atmosphere is a functional thing in a church'; this view was endorsed by Edward Mills, who commented: 'Planning problems in many church projects are the least important ... the creation of an appropriate atmosphere is the problem which faces the architect.' Spence 1956, pp.369, 375.

15 See Frances Spalding,'John Piper and Coventry, in war and peace', *Burlington Magazine*, July 2003, p.495.

16 Nikolaus Pevsner, *The Englishness of English Art*, London 1956, pp.125–6.

17 Henry-Russell Hitchcock, 'English Architecture in the Early 1960s', *Zodiac*, vol.12, 1964, pp.34–9. The article was largely devoted to Spence's work.

18 Letter from Spence to Gorton, 23 July 1955, Sir Basil Spence Archive RCAHMS.

19 A timber cross was meant to stand in a rock garden – symbolising the Garden of Gethsemane – outside the east end of the church. The source of the motif is the Finnish chapel of Otaniemi (K. and H.Siren, 1956); Eliel Saarinen's Church Lutheran in Minneapolis (1950) pioneered the cranked wall motif.

20 Edward Mills, 'Cathedral and churches by Basil Spence', *Architect and Building News*, 21 May 1958, p.674. The author is indebted to Clive B. Fenton and David Walker's research on Spence's parish church and chapel designs.

21 See Spence 1956.

22 See Mills 1958 for a perspective of the Edinburgh chapel.

23 Fiberglass windows designed by Piper were set into the walls, a pyramid skylight over the sanctuary, and hidden light from windows in baptistery and vestry. See 'St Matthew's Church, Reading', *Building*, 18 February 1968.

24 Spence's Edinburgh partner Hardie Glover detailed the building.

25 An early sketch for the Sussex University chapel reproduced in James Dunnett, 'Spence's personal

works', *Architects Journal*, 15/22 August 1996, p.24, shows split buttresses. Dunnett provides a perceptive analysis of Spence's late religious buildings.

26 See J.L.Tarn, 'Liverpool's two cathedrals' in Diana Wood (ed.), *The Church and the Arts*, Oxford, 1992, pp.537–69. The Vatican Council in 1963 passed measures increasing lay participation in the liturgy; from 1964 new Catholic churches in England had to position the altar free of the eastern wall. See E. Harwood, 'Liturgy and architecture: the development of the centralised eucharistic space', *Twentieth Century Architecture 3: The Twentieth Century Church,* London, 1998.

Building for Modern Ceremony
Miles Glendinning
pages 77–85

1 For instance, see B. Bergdoll, *European Architecture 1750–1890*, Oxford, 2000, p.243; R. Dixon and S. Muthesius, *Victorian Architecture*, London, 1978, p.17.

2 See M. Glendinning, 'Teamwork or masterwork? The design and reception of the Royal Festival Hall', *Architectural History*, vol.46, 2003, pp.277–319.

3 E. Mumford, *The CIAM Discourse on Urbanism, 1928–1960*, Cambridge Mass., 2000, p.177.

4 *Builder*, 29 July 1955, pp.172–3. 'Project: Town Hall Extension, Slough', *Builder*, 10 May 1957, pp.856–7.

5 T. Rohan, 'The dangers of eclecticism: Paul Rudolph's Jewett Arts Center at Wellesley', in S. W. Goldhagen and R. Legault (eds), *Anxious Modernisms*, Montreal, 2000, pp.191–213.

6 *Docomomo New York/Tri-State Newsletter*, Summer 2004, p.1; R.A.M. Stern, T. Mellins, D. Fishman, *New York 1960*, New York, 1995 (1997 edn), pp.677–84.

7 Sir E. Shuckburgh, 'The British presence', *Architectural Review*, September 1971, p.155.

8 *Architectural Review*, September 1971, pp.149–70.

9 Sir Basil Spence Archive, RCAHMS. Spence to A. Clarke, 1 March 1961, May 1961, 18 August 1961.

10 *Daily Express*, 28 February 1969.

11 J. Loeffler, *The Architecture of Diplomacy*, New York, 1998, p.169.

12 B. Cherry and N. Pevsner, *London 2: South*, London, 1983 (2002 edn), pp.351–55.

13 Glendinning and Muthesius 1994, pp.132–47.

14 English Heritage, *Survey of London*, vol.45, London, 2000, pp.68–73; Sir Basil Spence Archive, RCAHMS, letter from Spence to War Office, 24 October 1960, letter of 2 November 1959 from War Office to Spence, 23 November 1959 from Gibson to Spence and reply of 25 November; Gibson, 'Imagination invades the War Office', *The Times*, 3 July 1961, supplement ('The architect in Britain today').

15 Interviews with Anthony Blee, 2004, and John Church, 2005; Sir Basil Spence Archive, RCAHMS, notes of 1957 for report of RFAC.

16 Sir Basil Spence Archive, RCAHMS, letter of 3 January 1961 from RFAC to War Office; letter of 29 March 1961 from Gibson to Spence; letter of 1 May 1961 from Richards to Blee and reply of 23 May; letter of 6 September 1962 from Richards to Spence and reply of 12 September.

17 Interview with A. Blee, 2004; Ministry of Defence, *Hyde Park Cavalry Barracks*, London, 1970; *Builder*, 2 August 1963, pp. 212–20.

18 E. Happold, 'The Reconstruction of the Hyde Park Cavalry Barracks', London, 1970, paper prepared for Public Works and Municipal Services Congress, 20 November 1970.

19 Ministry of Public Building and Works, Press Notice 307/1970, *Hyde Park Cavalry Barracks, Knightsbridge*, London 1970; interview with A. Blee, 2004; Astragal, *Architects' Journal*, 28 October 1970, p.997; *Building*, 12 April 1974, p.40; *Financial Times*, 21 October 1970, p.25.

From Genius Loci to the Gorbals
Miles Glendinning
pages 87–95

1 Bullock 2002, pp.199–216, 229–43; Glendinning and Muthesius 1994, pp.153–6.

2 A. Downs (ed.), *Peter Shepheard*, Redhill, 2004; A. Korn, 'A new plan for Amsterdam', *Architectural Review*, vol.83, 1938, pp.265–76.

3 *Architect and Building News*, 11 November 1949; *Architects' Journal*, 3 November 1949, 8 December 1949, 19 January 1950; *Architectural Review*, July 1953, p.45; *Architects' Journal*, 11 January 1953, p.18–20.

4 *Architect and Building News*, 26 March 1948.

5 Glendinning and Muthesius 1994, p.31.

6 *Architect and Building News*, 28 January 1959, p.109.

7 *Architectural Review*, May 1970, p.363; *Architect and Building News*, 6 May 1964, p.802.

8 Bullock 2002, pp.42–9, 277; Glendinning and Muthesius 1994, p.108.

9 *Builder*, 2 November 1951, pp.581–5, and 7 November 1952, pp.668–71; *Architectural Review*, December 1952, pp.396–7.

10 G. Vinken, 'Gegenbild, Traditionsinsel, Sonderzone – Altstadt im modernen Staedtebau', in I. Scheurmann and H. R. Meier (eds), *Echt, Alt, Schoen, Wahr – Zeitschichten der Denkmalpflege*, Deutscher Kunstverlag, Muenchen, 2006, pp.190–201.

11 *Builder*, March 1961, pp.886–8; *Architectural Design*, January 1962, p.43.

12 R. Chamberlain, *Architecture and Building*, April 1960, p.129; Glendinning and Muthesius 1994, p.132.

13 'Slabby pierced wall thing': Sir Basil Spence Archive, RCAHMS Edinburgh, letter from Spence to Ferguson, 4 May 1959.

14 R. Banham, *The New Brutalism*, London, 1966, p.130.

15 *Architect and Building News*, 28 April 1950.

16 M. Horsey, *Tenements and Towers*, Edinburgh, 1990, p.39; Glendinning and Muthesius 1994, p.170. *Surveyor*, 6 September 1958, pp.890–1; *Official Architect*, October 1958, pp.469–72.

17 National Archives of Scotland, file DD6–2152, letters from Jury to Fleming of March 1958.

18. *Architects' Journal*, 4 February 1960, pp.197–203; *Surveyor*, 13 May 1961, pp.615–16; *Architect and Building News*, 6 May 1964, p.792.

19 *Architectural Review*, November 1967, pp.348–9.

20 Glendinning and Muthesius 1994, p.327.

'Drawing a New Map of Learning'
Louise Campbell
pages 97–103

1 Nikolaus Pevsner, 'Universities: yesterday', *Architectural Review*, October 1957, p.234. Lionel Brett described Swansea as 'an academic subtopia of sprawling buildings amid the ruination of a handsome landscape', 'Universities: today', *Architectural Review*, October 1957, p.250.

2 This point is made by in Muthesius 2001, pp.104–5.

3 Gavin Stamp, 'Anti-Ugly', *Apollo*, January 2005, pp.88–90.

4 'Basil Spence and Queens' College Cambridge', *Prefabrication*, February 1958, p.150. According to hearsay, they destroyed the model of Dykes Bowers's design.

5 Nicholas Taylor, *Cambridge New Architecture*, Saffron Walden, 1965, p.28.

6 Letters of 3, 4, 5, 6 and 10 February 1958.

7 'Undergraduate rooms: Queens' College, Cambridge', *Architectural Review*, July 1961, p.52.

8 See Taylor 1965 (note 5), pp.10–11.

9 See W.G. Stone, 'Steps leading to the foundation of the University', in D. Daiches 1964, p.192. Muthesius 2001, p.110, identifies them as Holford, Casson, Martin, Sheppard and Spence.

10 The University Grants Committee did not provide funding for residences at this stage, and Brighton guest-houses were regarded as the chief source of student accommodation.

11 On 21 August 1963 Fulton's secretary sent Spence a photo of the two men taken during the Installation ceremony: 'It is, I think, rather a good study of the two architects of the university' she wrote. Sir Basil Spence Archive, RCAHMS.

12 Basil Spence, 'Building a New University' in Daiches 1964, p.206.

13 Ibid., p.201.

14 Letters between Spence and Crowe exchanged in March and May 1962 agree that she should provide advice on tree thinning, contouring, new planting and the location of paths and roads. Her report with recommendations was dated 28 November 1962,

Sir Basil Spence Archive, RCAHMS.

15 Spence referred to the 'hinterland of huts and red-brick blocks' at Southampton, which he attempted to pull together with an engineering tower, quoted in Muthesius 2001, p.62.

16 Keele, founded 1947, was technically the first post-war new university, but got its charter a year after Sussex, in 1962; the main buildings, set in the grounds of Keele Hall, were unrelated in style and materials, and – with the exception of Pace's chapel – architecturally undistinguished.

17 Spence 1962, p.95.

18 'Influences of Greek and Roman architecture in the proposed Sussex University', Architect and Building News, 13 April 1960, p.471.

19 See P.K. Skriver, 'L'Universita di Aarhus – un progetto di lunga durata', Casabella, 1991, pp.46–63.

20 Winchester recalls the shape of the arches being intensively discussed, with influences from the great arcaded Piazza Ducale at Vigevano, and from Corbusier's Maisons Jaoul and his Roq et Rob schemes. Interview, April 2004. Paoletti recalls the impact of Gordon Cullen's townscape drawings in the Architectural Review. Interview, November 2006.

21 Spence in Daiches 1964, p.210.

22 An initial cohort of fifty students was admitted in 1961 and taught in rented accommodation in Brighton.

23 Spence explained that 'the rounded forms and the prefabricated arched form which had membranes for lifting and moving were made on the site, where we had a little out-door factory erected – this was the genesis for the building'. 'Sir Basil Spence, O.M., on his work from a broadcast interview by John Donat, Listener, 18 January 1965, p.254. See also R.M.E. Diamant, 'Precast structure at Sussex University', Architect and Building News, 19 December 1962, pp. 924–6.

24 See 'Sussex University', Architects' Journal Information Library, 30 October 1963, pp.891–910. 'Influences' 1960 (see note 18), p. 471.

25 Asa Briggs, 'Drawing a new map of learning' in Daiches 1964, p.76. The European Foundations – featuring the civilisations of classical antiquity – was a core course for arts undergraduates in the School of European Studies; science undergraduates studied a course in the history of science. See the University Curriculum, reproduced as Appendix A, pp.226 and 48.

26 See Muthesius 2001, p.114.

27 It had originally been agreed that 3,000 students should be taken by 1970.

28 Dennis Cox, in 'The Library of a New University' in Daiches 1964, describes the idea of providing informal reading areas and carrels instead of a monumental reading room, 'a building of quiet attractive comfort', p.156.

29 Spence in Daiches 1964, p.207.

30 'Memorandum on the Proposed Fine Arts Centre in the University of Sussex', July 1962, Sir Basil Spence Archive, RCAHMS, provides a fascinating rationale for an Arts Centre.

31 Fitzroy Robinson designed the Refectory and H. Hubbard Ford and Ronald Sims the first halls of residence.

32 'Influences' 1960 (see note 18), p.471, and Spence in Daiches 1964.

33 Interview with Spence in Interior Design, November-December 1960, p.73.

34 Spence in 1965 wrote: 'one realizes that students at Sussex wear jeans, and they have beards and longish hair, and this is the sort of environment I would like to see them in, with cushions in bright, random colours, which they can take up and throw on the floor and sit on, and all the furniture is very robust and strong' Spence in Donat 1965, p.255. And of Falmer House Junior Common Room, Spence wrote: '[students] must not feel as if the walls would take on damage. Hence the walls are brick. The floors are oak. And there was no paintwork. It was practically indestructible. And this furniture we designed – I felt it should be strong and robust, so that if a student kicked it, the student retired limping': B. Spence, 'The planning and building of the University of Sussex', Proceedings of the Royal Institution of Great Britain, vol.41, no.189, 1966, p.211. In 1967 he wrote of Falmer House as 'the father and mother building for students and staff': Sir Basil Spence, 'University of Sussex', in Brawne 1967, p.27.

35 Spence described College House [i.e. Falmer House] in a draft article of around 1962 as containing 'a series of communicating spaces on two levels – a rather noble expression of the university idea', Sir Basil Spence Archive, RCAHMS.

36 'University of Sussex', typescript, n.d., p.2, Sir Basil Spence Archive, RCAHMS. In 1967, Spence wrote: 'I think we owe it to the students that they should go away with the experience that they have been at a university where there is a consistent feeling of enclosure, and … of having been cosseted in the architectural sense … It should leave a lasting visual memory', Brawne 1967, p.27.

37 Peter Chamberlain, 'Integrating town and gown', The Times, 'The Architect in Britain Today', 3 July 1961, p. ix.

38 Of red-brick, Mary Scrutton wrote disdainfully: 'At every level there is a strong temptation to fraud and Lucky Jimmery'. Quoted in 'Universities', Architectural Review, 1957, p.240.

39 Taylor 1965 (see note 5), pp.110–13.

40 See E. Harwood, England: a guide to post-war listed buildings, London, 2003, p.283 and, for example, in the fantastic concrete vaulted hall at Denys Lasdun's Fitzwilliam College Cambridge.

Photographic & Copyright Credits

Illustrations in the text accompanied by a RCAHMS catalogue number indicate a reproduction of a photograph from the collection of the Royal Commission on the Ancient and Historical Monuments of Scotland. Where there is no RCAHMS number, the image is from another collection. The RCAHMS catalogue number does not necessarily indicate that the original material reproduced (such as a design or a model) is in the collection of the RCAHMS. Further details may be obtained from the RCAHMS, see Sources, p.123.

Henk Snoek: front cover, inside front cover, p.8, 44, 51–2, 65, 67, 69, 70, 73–4, 85–6, 100, 110, 114, 116, 119, 120–3

National Railway Museum / SSPL: frontispiece, 26

Fox Photos, London: 6

Publifoto, Rome: 8

Gillian Blee: 9

Anthony Blee: 10–13, 59, 62, 105, 136

Courtesy of Barratts Photo Press Limited: 24, 70, 133

Condé Nast Publications Limited: 28, 44

Courtesy of Scottish Field: 43

Country Life: 47, 48

Elain Harwood: 80

Louise Campbell: 81

Axel Poignant: 86

Eric de Maré: 118

Courtesy of John Laing and Son Limited: 173

Every effort has been made to trace the copyright holders, but if any have been inadvertently overlooked the publishers will be pleased to make any necessary arrangements at the first opportunity.